WONDROUS
LOVE

UPDATED EDITION

Register This New Book

Benefits of Registering*

- ✓ FREE **replacements** of lost or damaged books
- ✓ FREE **audiobook** – *Pilgrim's Progress,* audiobook edition
- ✓ FREE information about new titles and other **freebies**

www.anekopress.com/new-book-registration

*See our website for requirements and limitations.

WONDROUS
LOVE

GOD'S LOVE FOR A WORLD OF LOST SINNERS

DWIGHT L. MOODY

CONTENTS

Ch. 1: Picturing Christ's Boundless Compassion 1

Ch. 2: The New Birth 17

Ch. 3: The Importance of Blood 31

Ch. 4: Christ Is Our All in All 55

Ch. 5: Naaman the Syrian 75

Ch. 6: One Word – Gospel 89

Ch. 7: The Way of Salvation 105

Ch. 8: The Eight "I Wills" of Christ 121

Ch. 9: The Right Kind of Faith 137

Ch. 10: The Dying Thief 151

Dwight L. Moody – A Brief Biography 161

Other Similar Titles 163

A compilation of sermons that Mr. Moody preached in London, in the late 19th century.

WONDROUS LOVE

By Martha M. Stockton

God loved the world of sinners lost
    And ruined by the fall;
Salvation full, at highest cost,
    He offers free to all.

Oh, 'twas love, 'twas wondrous love,
    The love of God to me;
It brought my Savior from above,
    To die on Calvary!

E'en now by faith I claim Him mine,
    The risen Son of God;
Redemption by His death I find,
    And cleansing through the blood.

Love brings the glorious fulness in,
    And to His saints makes known
The blessed rest from inbred sin,
    Through faith in Christ alone.

Believing souls, rejoicing go;
    There shall to you be given
A glorious foretaste, here below,
    Of endless life in heaven.

Of victory now o'er Satan's power
    Let all the ransomed sing,
And triumph in the dying hour
    Through Christ, the Lord, our King.

CHAPTER I

PICTURING CHRIST'S BOUNDLESS COMPASSION

*And Jesus went forth, and saw a great multitude,
and was moved with compassion toward them,
and He healed their sick.* – Matthew 14:14

It is often recorded in Scripture that Jesus was moved by compassion, and we are told in this verse that after the disciples of John had come to Him and told Him that their master had been beheaded, that he had been put to a cruel death, Jesus went out into a desert place, and the multitude followed Him, and when He saw the multitude He had "compassion" on them, and healed their sick. If He were here in person, His heart would be moved as He looked down into your faces because He could also look into your hearts and could read the burdens and troubles and sorrows you have to bear. They are hidden from my eyes, but He knows all about them, and when the multitude gathered round about Him, He knew how many weary, broken and aching hearts were there.

He is also here tonight, and although we cannot see Him with our eyes, there is not a sorrow or trouble or affliction which any of you are enduring but He knows all about it. He is the same tonight as He was when here upon earth – the same Jesus, the same Man of compassion. When He saw that multitude, He had compassion on it and healed their sick, and I hope He will heal a great many sin-sick souls and bind up a great many broken hearts.

And let me say that no matter how bruised and broken your heart is, the Son of God will have compassion upon you, if you will let Him. *He will not break a bruised reed, nor quench the smoking flax* (Matthew 12:20). He came into the world to bring mercy and joy and compassion and love.

If I were an artist, I should like to draw some pictures and put before you that great multitude on which He had compassion.

THE LEPER HEALED

I would draw a painting of that man coming to Him full of leprosy, full of it from head to foot. There he was, banished from his home, banished from his friends, and he comes to Jesus with his sad and miserable story. And now, my friends, let us make the Bible stories real, for that is what they are. Think of that man. Think how much he had suffered. I don't know how many years he had been away from his wife and children and home, but there he was. He had put on strange and particular clothing, so that anybody coming near him might know that he was unclean, and when he saw anyone approaching him he had to raise the warning cry, "Unclean! Unclean! Unclean!"

And if the wife of his bosom were to come out to tell him that a beloved child was sick and dying, he dared not come near her. He was obliged to flee. He might hear her voice at a distance, but he could not be there to see his child in its last dying moments. He was, as it were, in a living tomb. It was worse than death. There he was, dying by inches, an outcast from everybody and everything, and not a hand put out to relieve him. Oh, what a terrible life!

Then think of him coming to Christ, and when Christ saw him, it says He was moved with compassion. He had a heart that beat in sympathy with the poor leper. He had compassion on him, and the man came to Him and said, "Lord, if You will it, you can make me clean." He knew there was no one to do it but the Son of God Himself, and the great heart of Christ was moved with compassion toward him. Hear the gracious words that fell from His lips: "I will it – be clean!" The leprosy is banished, and the man is made whole immediately.

Look at him now on his way back home to his wife and children and friends! He is no longer an outcast, no longer a loathsome thing, no longer cursed with that terrible leprous disease, but going back to his friends rejoicing. Now, my friends, you may say you pity a man who was so badly off, but did it ever strike you that you are a thousand times worse off? The leprosy of the soul is far worse than the leprosy of the body. I would rather a thousand times have the body full of leprosy than go down to hell with the soul full of sin. A good deal better that this right hand of mine were lopped off, that this right foot should decay and that I should go halt and lame and blind all the days of my life than be banished from God by the leprosy of sin.

Hear the wailing and the agony and the woe that is going up from this earth caused by sin! If there is one poor, sin-sick soul filled with leprosy here tonight, if you come to Christ, He will have compassion on you and say, as He did to that man, "I will – be clean."

THE DEAD ARE RAISED

Now we come to the next picture that depicts Him moved with compassion. Look into a little home where a poor widow is sitting. Perhaps a few months before she had buried her husband, and now she has an only son. How she dotes on him! She looks to him to be her stay, her support and her friend in old age. She loves him far better than her own lifeblood. But at last sickness enters the home, and death comes with it and lays his ice-cold hand upon the young man. You can see the widowed mother watching over him day and night, but at last his eyes are closed, and the loved voice is hushed, she thinks, forever. She will never see or hear him again after he is buried out of her sight.

And so, the hour comes for his burial. Many of you have been in the house of mourning and have been with your friends when they have gone to the grave and looked at the loved one for the last time. There is no one here, I dare say, who has not lost a loved one. I never went to a funeral and saw a mother take the last look of her child but it has pierced my heart, and I could not keep back the tears. Well, the mother kisses her only son on that poor, icy forehead. It is her last kiss, her last look. The body is covered up, and they put him on the bier and start for the place of burial. She had a great many friends, and the little town of Nain was moved at the sight of the widow's only son being borne away.

Look at that great crowd as they come pushing out of the gates, but over there are thirteen men, weary, dusty, and tired, and they have to stand aside to let the great crowd pass. The Son of God is in this group, and the others with Him are His disciples. He looks upon the scene and sees the mother with her broken heart, sees it bleeding, crushed, and wounded, and it touches His heart. The great heart of the Son of God is moved with compassion, and He comes up, touches the bier, and says, "Young man, rise up!" and the young man comes forth.

I can see the multitude startled and astonished. I can see the widowed mother rejoicing as she returns from the grave with the morning rays of the resurrection shining in her heart. He indeed had compassion on her, and there is not a widow reading this but Christ's voice will respond to your trouble and give you peace.

Let me say to you whose hearts are aching, you need a friend like Jesus. He is just the friend the widow needs. He is just the friend every poor, bleeding heart needs. He will have compassion on you and will bind up your wounded, bleeding heart if you will only come to Him just as you are. He will pull you to his loving bosom without scolding or chastising and say, "Peace, be still." You can walk in the unclouded sunlight of His love from this night. Christ will be worth more to you than all the world. He is just the friend that all of you need, and I pray God you may every one of you know Him from this hour as your Savior and friend.

A STRANGER'S COMPASSION FOR A MAN WHO WAS ROBBED AND BEATEN

The next picture which I show you to illustrate Christ's compassion is the man who was going to Jericho and fell among thieves. They took his coat and if he had a watch they would have taken that as well. They took his money and stripped him and left him half dead. See him wounded, bleeding, and dying.

A priest came down the road and looked upon the scene. His heart might have been touched, but he was not moved with enough compassion to help. He might have said, "Poor fellow," but he passed by on the other side and left him lying there. After him came a Levite, and he said, "Poor man," but he was not moved to help. There are a good many like the priest and Levite! Perhaps some of you have met a drunkard reeling in the street and just said "Poor fellow," or maybe you laughed because he stammered out something foolish. We are very unlike the Son of God.

At last a Samaritan came down, and he looked down on the man and had compassion on him. He got off his beast and took oil and poured it into his wounds and bound them up and took him out of the ditch, helpless as he was. He placed him on his own animal, brought him to an inn and took care of him. That good Samaritan represents your Christ and mine. He came into the world to seek and to save that which was lost.

Young man, have you come to London and fallen in with bad companions? Have they taken you to theaters and vicious places and left you bleeding and wounded? Come to the Son of God, and He will have compassion on you, take you off the dunghill, transform you and lift you up into His kingdom and into the heights of His glory if you will only let Him!

I do not care who you are. I do not care what your past life may have been. As He said to the poor woman caught in adultery, "Neither do I condemn you: go, and sin no more." He had compassion upon her, and He will have compassion on you. That man coming down from Jerusalem to Jericho represents thousands in London, and that good Samaritan represents the Son of God. Young man, Jesus Christ has set His heart on saving you. Will you receive His love and compassion? Do not have such hard thoughts about the Son of God. Do not think He has come to condemn you. He has come to save you.

THE RETURN OF THE PRODIGAL SON

I would like to draw another picture, another scene – the young man going away from his home that we read of in Chapter 15 of Luke. This is an ungrateful man, as ungrateful a wretch as anyone ever saw. He could not wait for his inheritance till his father was dead. He wanted his share at once and said to his father, "Give me the goods that belong to me," and his kind father gives him the goods and away he goes.

I can see him now as he starts his journey full of pride, boastful and arrogant, and goes out in grand style to see life in some foreign country, for instance going down to London. How many have come down to London, that being a far country to them, and squandered all their money? He was a popular man as long as he had money, and his friends lasted as long as his money did. He was a very popular young man in London, a "hail fellow well met" everywhere he went. He always paid the liquor bill and bought cigars.

Yes, he had plenty of friends in London. What grand folly! When his money was gone, where were his friends? You that serve the devil have a hard master! When the prodigal's money was all gone, they laughed at him and called him a fool, and so he was. What a blind, misguided young man he was! Just see what he lost. He lost his father's home, his table, food, reputation, and every comfort, and he lost his work, except what he got for feeding pigs. He was in an unlawful business. And that's just what someone who repudiates his faith – a backslider – is doing: He is in the devil's pay. You are losing your time and good name. No one has any confidence in a backslider, for even worldly people despise such a character.

This young man lost the reputation of his family name. Among the disreputable people in that foreign country, someone finally came along and, taking his measure, said, "Look at that miserable, wretched, dirty, barefooted man taking care of pigs."

"Don't talk to me like that," says the prodigal. "My father's a rich man and has servants better dressed than you."

"Don't tell me that," says the other man. "If you had such a father as that, I know very well he wouldn't claim you."

No one would believe him. He was no longer trustworthy. No one believes a traitor to his faith. Let him talk about his enjoyment with God, nobody believes it. Oh, poor backslider, I pity you! You had better come home again, and at last the poor prodigal came to himself and said, "I will go to my father." He started on the journey, and look at him as he goes along, pale and hungry with his head down, his strength exhausted, perhaps sick and so shattered that no one would know him but his father.

But love seeks its object, and the old man has often longed for his return. I imagine him up on the house-top on many nights hoping to catch a glimpse of him. On many long nights he has wrestled with God, asking that his prodigal son might come back. Everything he had heard from that country told him that his boy was going to ruin as fast as he could go. The old man spent much time in prayer for him, and at last faith began to rise up, and he said, "I believe God will send back my boy," and one day the old man saw in the distance his long-lost son.

He did not know him by his dress, but he knew his walk, and he said to himself, "Yes, that's my boy," and I can see him now running down the stairs and rushing along the highway, and that is just like God. Many times in the Bible God is represented as running. He is in a great hurry to meet his Son. He is running as the old man is running, seeing his child in the distance, and he has compassion on him.

The boy wanted to tell his father what he had done and where he had been, but the old man could not wait to hear him, his heart was so full of compassion, and he took him to his loving bosom. The boy wanted to go down into the kitchen, but the old man would not let him. He told the servants to put shoes on his feet, a ring on his finger, kill the fatted calf, and make merry. The prodigal had come home, the wanderer returned, and the old man rejoiced over the son's return.

Oh, backslider, come home, and there will be joy in your heart and in the heart of God. May God bring the backsliders back tonight – this very hour. Say, as the poor prodigal did, "I will rise up and go to my father," and on the authority of God I tell you God will receive you. He will blot out your sins and restore you to His love, and you will walk again in the light of His reconciled countenance.

CHRIST WEEPS FOR JERUSALEM

Let's look now at Jesus as he comes to mount Olivet under the shadow of the cross. The city bursts into view. He sees the Temple in all its grandeur and glory. The people are shouting, "Hosanna to the Son of David!" They are breaking off the palm branches, taking off their garments and spreading them on the ground before Him and bowing down before him, still shouting, "Hosanna to the Son of David!"

But He forgets it all. Even Calvary with all its sorrow He forgets. Gethsemane lay there at the foot of the hill, and He forgot it too. As He looked upon the city which He loved, the great heart of the Son of God was moved with compassion, and He cried aloud, "Oh, Jerusalem, Jerusalem, you who kill the prophets and stone the ones who are sent to you, how often I wanted to gather your children together, as a hen gathers her chick under her wings, and you would not let me!"

Imagine Him there, weeping over Jerusalem. What a wonderful city it might have been. How exalted to heaven it could have been if they had only known the day of their visitation and received instead of rejected their king. What a blessing He would have been to them!

Oh, poor backslider, behold the Lamb of God weeping over you, crying for you to come to Him and receive shelter and refuge from the storm that will sweep over this earth!

TAKING A LOOK AT POOR PETER

Peter denied the Lord and swore he never knew Him. If ever Christ needed sympathy, if ever He needed His disciples round

Him, it was that night when the rulers were bringing false witnesses against Him so that He might be condemned to death. And there was Peter, one of His foremost disciples, swearing he never knew Him.

The Lord might have turned on Peter and said, "Peter, is it true you don't know me? Is it true you have forgotten how I cured and healed your wife's mother when she lay at the point of death? Is it true you have forgotten how I raised you up when you were sinking in the sea? Is it true, Peter, you forgot how you were with me on the Mount of Transfiguration, when heaven and earth came together, and you heard the voice speaking from the clouds? Is it true you have forgotten that mountain scene when you wanted to build the three tabernacles? Is it true, Peter, you have forgotten me?"

Yes, He might have taunted poor Peter in this way, but instead of that He just gave him one look of compassion that broke Peter's heart and sent him out weeping bitterly.

COMPASSION FOR SAUL THE PERSECUTOR

Consider Saul, the bold blasphemer and persecutor who was going to stamp out the early church and was breathing threats and slaughter when Christ met him on his way to Damascus. It is the same Jesus still. Listen, and hear Him when He says, "Saul, Saul, why do you persecute Me?"

Jesus could have struck him down with a look or a breath but instead the heart of the Son of God was moved with compassion, and He cried out, "Saul, Saul, why do you persecute Me?"

If there is a persecutor here tonight, I would ask you, "Why persecute Jesus?" He loves you, sinner. He loves you, persecutor. You never received anything but goodness and kindness and love from Him.

Saul cried out, "Who are you?" And He answered, "I am

Jesus, who you are persecuting." It is hard to fight against such a loving friend, to contend against one who loves you as Jesus does, and down upon his face comes the proud Saul, and he cried out, "Lord, what would You have me do?"

The Lord told him, and Saul did it. May the Lord have compassion upon the unbeliever, and the skeptic and the persecutor. Let me ask you, my friend, is there any reason why you should hate Christ, or why your heart should be turned against Him?

I remember a story about a teacher telling the scholars to follow Jesus, and how they might all be missionaries and go out to work for others. And one day one of the smallest came to her and said, "I asked such and such a one to come with me, and they said they would like to come, but their father was an unbeliever." The young child wanted to know what an unbeliever was, and the teacher explained it to her. One day, when she was on her way to school, this particular man was coming out of the post office with his letters in his hand. She ran up to him, and said, "Why don't you love Jesus?"

He thought at first to push her aside, but the child pressed it home again.

"Why don't you love Jesus?" she asked.

If it had been another man, this man would have resented it, but he did not know what to do with the child.

She asked him again, with tears in her eyes, "Oh! please, tell me, why don't you love Jesus?"

He went on to his office, but he felt as if every letter he opened read, "Why don't you love Jesus?" He attempted to write with the same result. Every letter seemed to ask him, "Why don't you love Jesus?" He threw down his pen in despair and went out of his office, but he could not get rid of the question. It was asked by a still small voice within, and as he walked along it seemed as if the ground and the heavens whispered to him, "Why don't you love Jesus?"

At last he went home, and there it seemed as if his own children asked him the question, so he said to his wife, "I will go to bed early tonight," thinking he could sleep it away. But when he laid his head on the pillow it seemed as if the pillow whispered it to him. So he got up about midnight and said, "I can find out where Christ contradicts Himself, and I'll search it out and prove Him a liar."

The man got up, turned to the Gospel of John and read from the beginning until he came to the words, "God so loved the world that He gave His only begotten Son, that whosoever believes in Him should not perish, but have everlasting life." What love! he thought, and at last the old infidel's heart was stirred. He could find no reason for not loving Jesus, and down he went on his knees and prayed. Before the sun rose, that unbeliever was in the kingdom of God.

I will challenge any one on the face of the earth to find any reason for not loving Christ. It is only here on earth men that think they have a reason for not doing so. In heaven they know Him, and they shout, "Worthy is the Lamb that was slain." Oh, sinner, if you knew Him you would have no wish to find a reason for not loving Him. He is "chief among ten thousand and altogether lovely." I can imagine a good many people saying, "I should like very much to become a Christian, and I should like to know how I can come to Him and be saved."

For twenty years I have made this a rule. Christ is just as habitually near and as personally present to me as any other person living. When I have any troubles, trials, and afflictions, I go to Him with them. When I want counsel, I go to Him just as if I could talk face to face with Him. Twenty years ago God met me one night and took me to His bosom, and I would sooner give up my life tonight than give up Christ or that I should leave Him or that He should leave me, and that I should have no one to bear my burdens or tell my sorrows to.

He is worth more than all the world, and tonight He will have compassion upon you as He had upon me. I tried for weeks to find a way to Him. I finally just went and laid my burden upon Him, and He revealed Himself to me. I have ever since found Him a true and sympathizing friend, just the friend you need. Go right straight to Him. You need not go to this man or that man, to this church or that church. *I am the way, the truth, and the life* (John 14:6).

MERCY FOR THE SLEEPING SENTINEL

There are few names so dear to the Americans as that of Abraham Lincoln, and in an audience like this in America you would see the tears trickle down many cheeks at his name. He is very dear to us Americans. Do you want to know the reason why? I will tell you. He was a man of compassion. He was very gentle and was noted for his heart of sympathy for the down-trodden and the poor. No one went to him with a tale of sympathy but he had compassion on them, no matter how far down they were in the scale of society. He always took an interest in the poor.

There was a time in our history when we thought he had too much compassion. Many of our soldiers did not understand army discipline, and a great many were not true to army regulations. They intended to be, but they did not understand them, and many men consequently went wrong, were court-martialed and condemned to be shot, but Abraham Lincoln would always pardon them. At length, the nation rose up against him, and said that he was too merciful and, ultimately, they got him to declare that if a man was court-martialed he must be shot. There would be no more reprieves.

A few weeks after this, a young soldier was caught sleeping at his post. He was court-martialed and condemned to death. The boy wrote to his mother, "I do not want you to think I do not love my country, but it came about in this way: My comrade was sick, and I went out on picket for him, and the next night he ought to have come, but still being sick, I went out for him again and without intending it I fell asleep. I did not intend to be disloyal."

It was a very touching letter, and the mother and father said there was no chance to save him because there would be no more reprieves. But a little girl in that home knew that Abraham Lincoln had a little boy and knew that he loved that little boy. She said that if Abraham Lincoln knew how her father and mother loved her brother, he would never allow him to be shot. She took the train to Washington to plead for her brother. When she got to the White House, she first had to get past the guard at the gate. She told him her story, the tears ran down his cheeks, and he let her pass. But she next had to get past the secretary and some other officials, but she succeeded in getting into his private room, where senators and ministers were busy with State affairs.

The president saw the girl and called her to him. He said, "My child, what can I do for you?" and she told him her story. The big tears rolled down his cheeks, for he was a father, and his heart was touched. He treated the girl with kindness, reprieved the boy and gave him thirty days furlough to go home to see his mother. His heart was full of compassion.

Yet let me tell you, Christ's heart is more full of compassion than any man's. You are condemned to die for your sins, but if you come to Him, He will say, *Loose him, and let him go* (John 11:44).

He will rebuke Satan, and the dead shall live. Go to Him as that little girl went to the president and tell Him everything. Keep nothing from Him, and He will say, "Go in peace."

THE HAND OF COMPASSION

Let me ask the poor backslider: Did you ever feel the touch of the hand of Jesus? If so, you will know it again, for there is love in it. There is a story told in connection with our war of a mother who received a dispatch that her boy was mortally wounded. She went down to the front because she knew that the soldiers told to watch the sick and wounded could not watch her boy as she would.

She went to the doctor and said, "Would you like me to take care of my boy?"

The doctor said, "We have just let him go to sleep, and if you go to him the surprise will be so great it might be dangerous to him. He is in a very critical state. I will break the news to him gradually."

"But," said the mother, "he may never wake up. I should so dearly like to see him."

She so longed to see him that finally the doctor said, "You can see him, but if you wake him up and he dies, it will be your fault."

"Well," she said, "I will not wake him up if I may only go by his dying cot and see him."

She went to his side, and as she gazed upon him she could not keep her hand off his pallid forehead, and she touched him gently. Love and sympathy were in that hand, and the moment the slumbering boy felt it, he said, "Oh, mother! Have you come?" He knew there was sympathy and affection in the touch of that hand.

If you, oh, sinner, will let Jesus reach out His hand and touch your heart, you, too, will find sympathy and love in His hand. The prayer in my heart is that every lost soul here may be saved, and come to the arms of our blessed Savior.

FROM THE HYMN "JESUS, MY SAVIOR, TO BETHLEHEM CAME"

Jesus, my Savior, to Bethlehem came,
   Born in a manger to sorrow and shame;
Oh it was wonderful, blest be His name,
   Seeking for me, for me.

   . . .

Jesus, my Savior, on Calvary's tree,
   Paid my great debt, and my soul He set free;
Oh, it was wonderful, how could it be!
   Dying for me, for me.

CHAPTER 2

THE NEW BIRTH

Except a man be born again, he cannot see the kingdom of God. – John 3:3

And without being born again, how can a man inherit the kingdom of God? He can't even get a glimpse of the kingdom of God except he be born again. I believe this is the most important subject that will ever come before us in this world. I don't believe there is any truth in the whole Bible so important as the truth brought out in the third chapter of the Gospel of John. It is the *A B C* of God's alphabet. If a man is unsound on regeneration, he is unsound on everything.

That is really the foundation stone, and he must get the foundation right. If he doesn't, what is the good of trying to build a house? Christ says plainly, "Unless a man is born again, he cannot see the kingdom of God." But although regeneration or the new birth is taught so plainly here, I don't believe there is any truth in the whole Bible about which there is such great darkness as this great truth. There are a great many people who are like the man whose blind eyes saw men as trees walking. Many Christians do not seem to be clear about the new birth.

BEING "BORN" AS A CHRISTIAN

Only this afternoon, as I was in the inquiry-room, a person came in, and I said, "Are you a Christian?"

"Why," she says, "of course I am."

"Well," I said. "How long have you been one?"

"Oh, sir, I was born one!"

"Oh! indeed, then I am very glad to take you by the hand. I congratulate you. You are the first woman I ever met who was born a Christian. You are more fortunate than others. They are born children of Adam."

She hesitated a little, and then tried to make out that, because she was born in England, she was a Christian. There are many who have the idea that because they are born in a Christian country they have been born of the Spirit. In this chapter of John, the new birth is brought out so plainly that if anyone will read it carefully and prayerfully, I think his eyes will soon be opened. That which is born of the flesh is flesh and remains flesh. That which is born of the Spirit is spirit and remains spirit.

So, when a man is born of God, he has God's nature. When a man is born of his parents, he receives their nature, and they received the nature of their parents, and you can trace it back to Adam. But when a man is born of God, or born from above, or born of the Spirit – that is the way the Holy Ghost puts it in that third verse – he receives God's nature, and then he leaves the life of the flesh for the life of the spirit.

Before I go on, I want to say one thing, and that is what this new birth, or being born of the Spirit, is not. A great many think they have been born again because they go to church. A great many say, "Oh, yes, I am a Christian. I go to church every

Sunday!" Let me say here that there is no one that goes to church so regularly in all London as Satan. He is always there before the minister, and he is the last one out of the church. There is no church or chapel in London where he is not a regular attendant.

The idea that he is only down in the slums and lanes and alleys of London is a false idea. He is wherever the Word is preached. It is his business to be there and snatch away the seed. Some of you may go to sleep, but he won't. Some of you may not listen to the sermon, but he will. He will be watching, and when the seed is just entering into some heart he will go and snatch it away.

BAPTIZED IS NOT BORN

Another person will say, "Oh, yes, I am a Christian because I was baptized." I want to say here that baptism is one thing, and being born again is another. You cannot say that a baptism is the new birth. Would you call that being born from above? You cannot baptize a man into the kingdom of God. Bear that in mind. If I could save men by baptizing them, you would not catch me preaching. Instead, I would get water and baptize them. That would be the quickest way. There would be no use in praying and pleading for men to flee from the wrath of God. You can never get people into the kingdom of God by baptism.

Baptism is all right in its place. I am not here tearing down church ordinances. I am talking about the new birth, and there are a great many, I believe, who are deceived on this one point, that because they have been baptized at some time in their lives they have become Christians. That is not the new birth. That is not being born from above and of the Spirit. Do not let Satan deceive you, my friends, for it is a very important truth. We want everyone to understand – and I hope the Spirit of God will make plain the difference – between baptism and being born of the Spirit.

JOINING THE CHURCH

There is another type that says, "Oh, yes, I became a Christian when I joined the church." That also is not being born again. What has that, being united with the church on earth, to do with the new birth? There are a great many in the church who are on their way to death and ruin. A great many church members have no hope of eternal life. One of the twelve that Christ chose to follow Him turned out a hypocrite and a traitor. He was not loyal to Christ at heart. Don't build your hope of heaven upon some profession of faith. You must be born of God.

Stop a minute and think and ask yourselves this question, "Have I been born again?" It is the most solemn question that will ever come before you down here, "Have I been born from above? Have I been born of the Spirit?" It is not making some new resolutions. You have made enough of them. I never met anyone who had not made some good resolutions in their life. It is not trying to do good. Some say, "I try to do the best I can, and I think it will come out all right."

What is that to do with the new birth and the new creation? God does not promise salvation to him who tries to do the best he can, but to him who believes, or who is born of the Spirit, for "unless a man is born again, he cannot see the kingdom of God."

I believe this new birth is instantaneous. I have met a great many people who cannot tell the day or the hour of their conversion, but there must have been a time when they passed from death unto life – when they were born of the Spirit. There must have been a time when their names were written in the Book of Life, though they may not be conscious of the day, or the hour, or the week, or the month, or the year. My friends, I beg of you, be sure that you have been born of the Spirit. Don't be deceived upon this one truth, because Christ Himself says, "Unless a man is born again, he cannot see the kingdom of God."

FLESH CANNOT SERVE GOD

As I said before, when I was born of my parents I received their nature. I received the nature of the flesh, and I cannot serve God in the flesh. *God is a Spirit; and they that worship Him must worship Him in spirit and in truth* (John 4:24). Before a man can worship God he must be born of God. He must be born of the Spirit. With this new birth, with this new life, he can serve God, and then the yoke is easy and the burden light. A man may as well try to fly to the moon as to serve God before he has been born of the Spirit. It is utterly impossible. The natural man is an enemy of God. His natural heart is at war with God. It always has been and always will be.

And not only that, you cannot make it better. God never mends, He creates anew. Therefore don't try to patch up that old Adam nature. God says, "It shall never come into my presence." He tells us how we are to come into His presence and how we are to get into His kingdom. This is worth keeping in mind. You cannot educate men into it, which is what the world is trying to do. He who climbs up by some other way than the Lord's way is the same as a thief and a robber. You had better be born into it in God's way.

We have a law in America that no man shall be president of the United States who has not been born on American soil. A great many Englishmen have come to America, and a great many men have come from all parts of the world, yet I have never heard one complain of that law. They say America has the right to say who shall be president. I come here to your country, and I do not complain because you have a queen to reign over you. What right have I to complain? Has not England a right to say who shall rule it, and who shall be its queen? Foreigners have no right to interfere. And I would like to ask you this question: Has not God a right to say who shall come into His kingdom, and how we shall come?

God tells us how we are to come into His kingdom, and that is by the new birth. We must be born from above, born of the Spirit, and then we get a nature that goes out toward God. If you take a drunk and put him on the pavement of heaven, he will not be happy there. The drunkard doesn't want heaven. What would he do there? He has no whisky to drink, and he has none of his old companions. What is he to do? He would say, "This is hell to me. I don't want to stay here." A man who cannot spend one Sabbath on earth among God's people, what is he to do with that eternal Sabbath, with those that have washed their robes and made them white in the blood of the Lamb?

A man must have a spiritual nature before he wants to go to heaven, and heaven cannot hold any attractions for a man until he is born of the Spirit.

MORAL PEOPLE ALSO NEED THE NEW BIRTH

Let us go back to the man to whom Christ said those words. I often rejoice He didn't say this to the woman at the well nor to Mary Magdalene. If He had said it to them, people would have said, "Oh, that poor woman needs to be converted, but I am a moralist. I don't need to be converted. Regeneration will do for harlots, thieves, and drunkards, but we moralists do not need it."

But to whom did Christ say it? He said it to Nicodemus. Who was he? He belonged to the house of bishops. Nicodemus, one of the church dignitaries, stood very high, as high as any man in Jerusalem except the high priest himself. He belonged to the seventy rulers of the Jews, and he was a doctor of divinity and taught the law. There is not one word of Scripture against him. He was a man who stood out before the whole nation as of pure and spotless character, yet what does Christ say to him? "Unless a man is born again, he cannot see the kingdom of God." I can see a scowl on his forehead.

He says, "What do you mean by being born again – born from above, born of the Spirit? Now I am old, can I enter my mother's womb a second time and be born again?"

Jesus says, "Truly, I say to you, unless a man is born of water and of the Spirit, he cannot see the kingdom of God."

He didn't take back what He had said – He repeated it. I can imagine Nicodemus was like tens of thousands of men in London today. The moment you talk to them about regeneration or conversion, there is a scowl on their forehead. They say, "I don't understand it." Of course the natural man doesn't understand spiritual things. It is a matter of revelation.

A great many men try to investigate and, in that way, find God. Suppose you spend a little of your time in asking God to reveal Himself to you.

REASON CAN'T COMPREHEND THE NEW BIRTH

I heard some time ago of commercial travelers who went to hear a man preach. They came back to the hotel and were sitting in the smoking room talking, and they said the minister did not appeal to their reason, and they would not believe anything they could not reason out. An old man who was sitting there listening said to them, "You say you won't believe anything you can't reason out?"

"No, we won't."

The old man said, "As I was coming in the train yesterday, I noticed some sheep, cattle, swine, and geese, all eating grass. Now, can you tell me by what process that same grass was turned into feathers, hair, bristles, and wool?"

"Well, no, we can't tell you that."

"Do you believe it is a fact?"

"Oh, yes, it is a fact."

"I thought you said you would not believe anything you could not reason out?"

"We can't help believing that. That is a fact we see before our eyes."

"Well," said the old man, "I can't help but believe in regeneration and a man being converted, although I cannot explain how God converted him."

CHRIST'S ILLUSTRATION OF THE WIND

The illustration which Christ used to Nicodemus was the wind. "The wind blows where it wants, and you hear the sound of it, but cannot not tell from where it comes or where it goes." You cannot see the Spirit of God work in this audience but I hope and pray He may be working now in the hearts of many and convincing them of sin! Do you believe more than ever that you are a sinner? That is the work of the Holy Spirit. The devil never told you that you are a sinner. He tries to make you believe that you are good enough. If you believe that you have sinned against God, that is the work of the Holy Spirit and he is at work here. We cannot see Him, but there are a great many who know He is here.

Suppose I should say, "I don't believe in the wind. It must be all imagination. I have lived thirty-seven years and have never seen the wind. It is folly for men to talk about the wind." I can just imagine that boy there saying, "I know more than that man. I know there is wind, because it blew my hat off into the mud today, and I have often felt it blowing in my face."

My friends, you have never felt the wind more than I have felt the Spirit of God. You have never seen the effects of the wind more than I have seen the effects of the Spirit of God, and of the working of the Holy Spirit, and there are hundreds of witnesses here who would testify the same thing. Yet this invisible power does its work in creation, and the mighty invisible power of God does its work effectively in the spiritual sphere. New life in Christ means breaking old fetters.

GOD CAN CHANGE THE DRUNKARD

It may be that I am talking now to some poor drunkard. When he comes into his house his children listen and hear by the footsteps that their father is coming home drunk, and they run away and hide from him as if he was some horrid demon. His wife begins to tremble. Many times that great, strong arm has been brought down on her weak, defenseless body. Many times she has carried marks from that man's violence. He ought to be her protector, support, and stay but he has become her tormentor, and his home is like hell upon earth. There is no joy there.

There may be one such tonight who hears the good news that he can be born again and receive a nature from heaven – receive the Spirit of God. God can give him power to hurl the infernal cup from him. God will give him grace to trample Satan under his feet, and the drunk will then become a sober man. Go to that house three months from now, and you will find it neat and clean. As you draw near that home you hear singing and not the song of the drunkard. That is gone. All things have become new. He has been born of God and is singing one of the songs of Zion, "Rock of Ages, cleft for me; Let me hide myself in Thee."

Or perhaps he is singing that good old hymn that his mother taught him when he was a little boy,

> "There is a fountain filled with blood
>   Drawn from Immanuel's veins,
> And sinners plunged beneath that flood
>   Lose all their guilty stains."

He has become a child of God, an heir of heaven. His children are climbing on his knee, and he has his arms round their necks. That dark home is now changed into a little Bethel on earth. God dwells there now. God has done all that, and that is regeneration – that is being born of the Spirit.

GOOD RESOLUTIONS ARE WORTHLESS

Some of you may have been saying, "I wish Mr. Moody would tell us how we are to become Christians, for he says that we cannot be Christians by trying to do good and by making new resolutions." Perhaps there have been many times you were at a meeting and resolved to turn over a new leaf, and you may now form another good resolution. If you do, you will break it.

What are you going to do? If it is a new birth you are to have, you will not create life. Can you bring life to the dead? All the wise men in London cannot do so. God alone is the author of life, and if you are to have the new birth, it must be God's work. When the Jubilee Singers were in the North of England my family went to see them, and my little boy asked why they didn't wash the black off their faces. I told him it was because they were born black. The Ethiopian cannot change his skin, nor the leopard his spots. You cannot save yourself. There is a man dying – can you put new life into him? Or can you raise up a dead body by saying, "Young man, arise"? That is the work of God. Your souls are dead in trespasses and sins, and only the Lord Jesus Christ can speak life.

THE BEGGAR AND THE PRINCE

I imagine some of you will say, "Can't I do anything?" Well, you can't. Salvation has been worked out for you by another. Many go all around the world in search of honor or possessions, but salvation is worth thousands of times more than anything earth can produce, and you can't get it by searching the world.

God has but one price for salvation. Do you want to know what it is? It is without money and without price.

Rowland Hill said that most auctioneers found they had hard work to get people up to their price, but that he had hard work to get people down to his. *For the wages of sin is death; but the gift of God is eternal life* (Romans 6:23). Who will have it now? I ask the young man, will you have this gift?

Suppose I was going over London Bridge and saw a poor, miserable beggar, barefoot, coatless, hatless, with hardly any rags to cover his nakedness, and only a few yards behind him there was the Prince of Wales with a bag of gold. The poor beggar was running away from him as if from a demon, and the prince was calling after him, "Oh, beggar! Here is a bag of gold!" We would say the beggar had gone mad to run away from a prince with the bag of gold.

Sinner, that is your condition. The Prince of Heaven wants to give you eternal life, and you are running away from Him.

THE DYING SOLDIER

Suppose you say, "If it is not by earnestly working, how am I to be saved?" I will say, "Scripture will tell you." Remember the illustration that Christ used with Nicodemus. You could not have a better. He took him to the remedy: *As Moses lifted up the serpent in the wilderness, even so must the Son of man be lifted up: that whosoever believeth in Him should not perish, but have eternal life* (John 3:14-15). Now there is the remedy.

How am I to be saved? By looking to Christ, just by looking. It's very cheap, isn't it? Very simple, isn't it? Just look away to the Lamb of God now and be saved. What says the great wilderness preacher? *Behold the Lamb of God, which taketh away the sin of the world* (John 1:29). You can say the whole plan of salvation is in two words, "giving" and "receiving." God gives, I receive.

I remember, after one of the terrible battles in the American Civil War – I was in the army, tending soldiers – and I had just laid down one night, past midnight, to get a little rest, when a man came and told me that a wounded soldier wanted to see me. I went to the dying man.

He said, "I wish you to help me to die."

I said, "I would help you to die if I could. I would take you on my shoulders and carry you into the kingdom of God if I could, but I cannot. However, I can tell you of One who can."

And I told him of Christ being willing to save him, and how Christ left heaven and came into the world to seek and to save that which was lost. I quoted promise after promise, but all was dark, and it almost seemed as if the shades of eternal death were gathering around his soul. I could not leave him, and at last I thought of this third chapter of John, and I said to him, "Look here, I am going to read to you now a conversation that Christ had with a man that went to Him when he was in your state of mind, and inquired what he was to do to be saved."

I read that conversation to the man, and he lay there with his eyes riveted upon me, and every word seemed to be going home to his heart, which was open to receive the truth. When I came to the verse where it says, *And as Moses lifted up the serpent in the wilderness, even so must the Son of man be lifted up: that whosoever believeth in Him should not perish but have eternal life* (John 3:14-15), the dying man cried, "Stop, sir. Is that really in there?"

"Yes, it is all here."

Then he said, "Won't you please read it to me again?"

I read it the second time. The dying man brought his hands together, and he said, "Bless God for that. Won't you please read it to me again?"

I read through the whole chapter, but long before the end of it he had closed his eyes. He seemed to lose all interest in the rest of the chapter, and when I got through it his arms were folded on his breast, he had a sweet smile on his face. Remorse and despair had fled. His lips were quivering, and I leaned over him and heard him faintly whisper, "As Moses lifted up the serpent in the wilderness, even so the Son of man must be lifted up: that whoever believes in Him should not perish but have eternal life."

He opened his eyes and fixed his calm, deathly look on me, and he said, "Oh, that is enough. That is all I want," and in a few hours he rested his dying head on the truth of those two verses, rode away on one of the Savior's chariots and took his seat in the kingdom of God.

Oh, sinner, you can be saved now if you will! Look and live. May God help everyone who is lost to look on the Lamb of God, which taketh away the sin of the world.

CHAPTER 3

THE IMPORTANCE OF BLOOD

And almost all things are by the law purged with
blood, and without the shedding of blood is no
remission. – Hebrews 9:22

N o man can give a satisfactory reason for the hope that is
in him if he is a stranger to the blood. At the very com-
mencement of the Bible we find reference made to the subject
in Genesis 3:21, *Unto Adam also and to his wife did the Lord*
God make coats of skins, and clothed them. In this verse we
get the first glimpse of blood. Certainly God could not have
clothed Adam and Eve with the skins of beasts unless He had
shed blood. Here, then, we have the innocent suffering for the
guilty – the doctrine of substitution in the garden of Eden.

God dealt with Adam in grace before He dealt in judgment.
Death came by sin – Adam had sinned, and the Lord came down
to make the way of escape. God came to him as a loving friend
and not to hurl him from the earth. Adam could have said to
Eve, "Though the Lord has driven us out of the garden of Eden,
He loves us," for the coat was a token of love. God put a lamp

of promise into Adam's hand before He drove him out, saying, "The offspring of the woman shall strike the serpent's head."

Did you ever think what a terrible state it would be if man was allowed to live forever in his lost, ruined state? It was from love that God drove Adam out of Eden and that he should not live for ever. God put the cherubim with a flaming sword there. But now Christ has taken the sword out of his hand and opened wide the gate so that we can come in and eat. Adam might have been in Eden ten thousand years and then be led astray by Satan, but now "our life is hidden with Christ in God." Man is safer with the second Adam out of Eden than with the first Adam in Eden.

Let us next turn to Genesis 4:4, *And Abel, he also brought of the firstlings of his flock and of the fat thereof. And the Lord had respect unto Abel and to his offering.* Cain and Abel were brought up outside of Eden and had the same parents, and both received the same instruction as to how they were to draw near to God, but Cain came in his own way while Abel came in the way God commanded. Cain said to himself, "I am not going to bring a bleeding lamb. Here is the grain and the beautiful fruit that I have raised by my industry. I'm sure it looks better than blood, and I'm not going to bring blood."

It was not that there was any difference between these two men, but in the offering that each brought. One came in the way God had marked out and the other in a way of his own. There are in the present day a great many just like that. They prefer what is agreeable to the eye, as Cain did his beautiful corn and fruit, and they do not like the doctrine of the blood of atonement.

Any religion that makes light of the blood is the work of the devil, even if an angel from heaven came down to preach salvation through some other means. Undoubtedly, on the morning of creation, God marked out the way that a man might come to Him. Abel walked in God's way, and Cain in his own. Perhaps Cain could not bear the sight of blood, and so he took that which God had cursed and laid it upon the altar.

There are many Cains in the church even now, and some are in the pulpit. They preach against the doctrine of the blood and say that we can get to heaven without it. From the time Adam went out of Eden there have been people like Abel and people like Cain. The Abels come by the way of the blood, the way God has marked out for us. The Cains come by their own way. They repudiate the blood and say it does not atone for sin. But it is better to take God's word than man's opinion.

Turn to Genesis 8:20, *And Noah builded an altar unto the Lord; and took of every clean beast, and of every clean fowl, and offered burnt offerings on the altar.* We have thus passed over the first two thousand years and have come to the second dispensation. The thought I want to call your attention to is this: The first thing Noah did when he got out of the ark was to build an altar and slay the animals, thus putting blood between him and his sin. The second dispensation is founded upon blood, and these animals were taken through the flood in the ark that they might illustrate the indispensable necessity of shedding blood.

ABRAHAM'S OFFERING OF ISAAC

Genesis 22:13 says, *And Abraham lifted up his eyes, and looked, and behold behind him a ram caught in a thicket by his horns: and Abraham went and took the ram, and offered him up for a burnt offering in the stead of his son.* God loved Abraham so much that He spared his son, but He so loved the world that He would not spare His own Son – He gave His own Son up freely for us all. It may be that from the top of that mountain Abraham saw a glorious sight – Christ going up Calvary carrying His cross. He saw the mountain peak sprinkled with blood, and he saw that sacrifices were to go on until the true Isaac made His appearance and offered Himself for us all. Abraham had the altar built, and he was ordered to take his only son and bind him and slay him. He bound the boy, and everything was ready. He took the knife and was about to sacrifice him because it was the will and command of God. He did not know what it meant, but he obeyed.

Would that there were more men like him now, ready to obey God in the dark without asking the reason why! The old man took his son, and he told him the secret that he had hidden from him throughout the journey – that God had told him to offer him up as a sacrifice. He bound the boy hand and foot and laid him on the altar, and just when he was about to stretch forth his hand, he heard a voice from heaven calling: "Abraham, Abraham, spare your son." God was more merciful to the son of Abraham than to His own, for He gave Him up freely for us all. He opened up to him the curtain of time and showed him Christ coming in the future. Abraham saw his sins laid on Christ and was glad.

THE BLOOD OF PASSOVER

In Exodus 12:13 we read: *And the blood shall be to you for a token on the houses where ye are: and when I see the blood, I will pass over you, and the plague shall not be upon you to destroy you.*

God did not say, "When I see your good deeds, when I see how you have prayed and wept and cried." No. He said, "When I see the blood, I will pass over you. The blood shall be a token." What was it saved those men? Was it their good resolutions or their works? It was the blood. "When I see the blood I will pass over you." Very likely when some of the lords and dukes and great men rode through Goshen and saw the Israelites sprinkling blood on their dwellings, they said that they never saw such foolishness and that they were spoiling their houses. They were to sprinkle the doorposts and lintels of their houses with the blood, but not the threshold. God would not have the blood trampled upon, but that is what is happening in the world of today.

Some preachers speak not of the death of Christ but His life because it is more pleasing to the natural ear. But the life of Christ may be preached for ever and it will not save any man if His death is left out.

A live lamb could not have kept death out of the houses of Goshen. God did not say that He wanted a live lamb at every door, but he wanted the lintels and doorposts sprinkled with the lamb's blood. People sometimes say, "If I were as good as that minister, who preached the gospel for fifty years," or "If I were as good as that mother, who did so and so for her children," but if we are behind the blood of God's Son, we are just as safe as any Christian that has ever walked the face of the earth.

It is not a long life of usefulness that makes men and women acceptable to God. We must work for Christ, but we get salvation as a gift and then begin to work because we cannot help it. All the work a person does before he becomes converted goes for nothing.

The little child down in Goshen behind the blood of the lamb was just as safe as Joshua or any man in the whole town. The angel of death passed by when he saw the blood. The tiny little fly in the ark with Noah was as safe as the elephant. It was the ark that saved equally the fly and the elephant, and it is the blood that saves the weakest and the strongest. When death came that night with his sword, he entered the palace of the prince and went into the houses of the great and mighty, and they all had to pay tribute to death, for the first-born in Egypt was struck down that night. The only thing that kept death out was death itself.

The only way that death can be met is by death. I have sinned and must die or get someone to die for me. The great question is: Have you got the token? If death should come after any one of us tonight, are we sheltered by the blood? That is the point. It is the blood that atones, not my good resolutions or prayers or position in society or what I have done, but what has been done by another. God looks for the token.

Take another illustration. Suppose a man wanted to go from London to Liverpool, and he got into a railway carriage. He would soon hear the guard running along the platform crying out for tickets. A man might be rich or he might be poor, black or white, he might be learned or unlearned, that was not what the guard wants to know, he wants to see the tickets because the ticket is the token. If you have a ticket, you pass.

There was no death where the blood was. The Egyptians looked at the Israelites killing a lamb and sprinkling the blood on the door-posts no doubt as very foolish, but not one house in the city escaped if the doorposts and lintels did not wear the blood, no matter who the inhabitants were, rich or poor. That night there was no difference. A wail was heard in every habitation where the blood had not been sprinkled, from the palace to the meanest hovel, but the blood kept death out everywhere it had been sprinkled. That showed clearly the truth that without shedding blood there is no remission of sin. Let no man or woman be guilty of laughing at this doctrine, that the blood of Jesus Christ cleanses us from all sin.

In the eleventh verse of the same chapter we read, *And thus shall ye eat it; with your loins girded, your shoes on your feet, and your staff in your hand; and ye shall eat it in haste: it is the Lord's passover* (Exodus 12:11). You lack power because you don't feed on the Lamb, and this is why there are so many weak Christians. The Lamb not only atones for our sins, but we are also to feed upon the Lamb. We have a wilderness journey before us, as did the children of Israel. After we are saved, we are to feed upon Christ. He is the true bread from heaven. If I don't feed my soul with the true bread from heaven, I am sickly and have no power to work for Christ. That is the reason, I believe, why so few in the church have power. Some people think if they get one glimpse of Christ, that is enough.

Some think highly of their dinner. Why shouldn't God's children think a good deal of their spiritual food? We should no more think of laying in spiritual food to last for ten years than we should bodily food. A good many people are living on stale manna. A man in Ireland said to his boy, "I want you to eat two breakfasts. Do you know why?" The boy said he understood one was for his body and the other for his soul. All Christians should similarly take two breakfasts, one for the soul and one for the body.

The Passover was to be the beginning of months for the Jews. *This month shall be unto you the beginning of months: it shall be the first month of the year to you* (Exodus 12:2). All the four hundred years that they had been in bondage went for naught because this was the first month of the year to them. And in like manner throughout all the years that we have served the devil, and all the time that we have been in Egypt, whatever good we may have done in this world is to be reckoned as naught. Everything dates back to the Passover night, to the time the blood was put upon the doorposts.

All the time we are serving the world goes for naught. If you have not come to Calvary, you are losing time. Everything you do on the wrong side of the cross counts for nothing. The first thing is to be saved by faith in Christ, and then we commence our pilgrimage to heaven. We don't start, as some people suppose, from the cradle to heaven. We start from the cross. We have a fallen nature that is taking us to hell. We must be born of the Spirit, sheltered by the blood, and then we become pilgrims for heaven.

Each man was to take a lamb for his house. *And if the household be too little for the lamb, let him and his neighbour next unto his house take it according to the number of the souls; every man according to his eating shall make your count for the lamb* (Exodus 12:4). The lamb was not too little for a household, but the household might be too little for the lamb. Christ was enough for every household, enough and to spare, and we ought to pray that salvation may come to every member of our households.

Let us next turn to Exodus 29:16, *And thou shalt slay the ram, and thou shalt take his blood, and sprinkle it round about upon the altar.* Even Aaron could not come to God until he sprinkled blood around the altar, and when the high priest went into the holy of holies, he had to take blood with him. Since Adam fell there has been no other way by which a man can approach God than by the blood. You cannot have an audience with God until you come in that appointed way. So it has been for six thousand years. When Adam fell in Eden, he broke the golden chain that linked humanity to the throne of God, but Christ came and made atonement for the fall.

Observe in Leviticus 8:23, *And he slew it; and Moses took of the blood of it, and put it upon the tip of Aaron's right ear, and upon the thumb of his right hand, and upon the great toe of his right foot.*

I used to read a passage like this and say it seemed absurd. I think I understand it now. The blood upon the ear means that we are to hear the voice of God. The unconverted man does not understand the voice of God, and we are told that when the voice of God was heard, the uncircumcised said that it thundered. They did not know the difference between God's voice and thunder. Without the blood we cannot hear the voice of God and understand it. A man must be sheltered by the blood before he can hear God's voice.

The blood upon the hand signifies that a man may work for

God. You cannot work for God until you are sheltered behind the blood. You may build churches, endow colleges, pay ministers and missionaries, but it all goes for naught until you are sheltered by the blood. Don't let anyone deceive you on this point. Don't let Satan deceive you by telling you that you can get to heaven by some other way. They asked Christ, "What must we do, that we may work the works of God?" Perhaps these men had pockets full of money and were ready and willing to build churches. Christ told them that the work of God was that they should believe in His Son, but they were not willing to do such a small thing. They would rather do some greater thing, but that was not wanted. You cannot do anything to please God until you believe.

"To obey is better than sacrifice," says Samuel. People may work day and night, and even work themselves to death, but they never will do right until they do what God requires them to do.

The blood on the toe of the right foot was to show that Aaron was to walk with God. When Adam fell, communion with God was broken. Before, he had walked with God but the moment he sinned he fell out of communion with Him, and from that time to this God has been trying to get man back into communion. God is full of truth and justice. His justice must be met and after that has been met, He is satisfied.

God never walked with men until He put them behind the blood at Goshen. What could stand before them then? They passed through the Red Sea, and God said to Joshua, "Take this country, and no man shall be able to stand before you all the days of your life." In the days of Joshua there were whole regiments of giants, but one stripling from the Lord's hosts defeated the giant of Gath. If God is with us, the giants will be like grasshoppers. If God is not with us, it will be different. I would rather have ten men separated from the world than ten thousand nominal Christians who go to the prayer meeting tonight and the ball tomorrow.

In Leviticus 16:14, it says: *He shall take of the blood of the bullock, and sprinkle it with his finger upon the mercy seat eastward; and before the mercy seat shall he sprinkle of the blood with his finger seven times.* It seems as if God originally gave Adam a life by which he held communion with Him, but on the day that he broke the command he lost that communion. Ever since, God has been trying to get men back into communion with Himself. But how could God be just and the justifier of sinners? That is done through the Blood of Christ.

"The life of the flesh is in the blood." God demands blood to atone for sin.

Man's life was forfeited, and he had to die. He had to pay the wages of death. He could not pay the penalty and live, so he wanted a substitute. Every man had sinned, and could not be a substitute for his fellow, but Christ was sinless and could become the substitute for man, and He has become that substitute. He has died in the place of man to satisfy the law. The question for each and every one to answer is whether they will love and serve Him who has died to redeem them by His precious blood.

In Leviticus 17:11, we read: *For the life of the flesh is in the blood: and I have given it to you upon the altar to make an atonement for your souls: for it is the blood that maketh an atonement for the soul.* Some may say, "Why does God demand blood?" and someone once said to me: "I detest your God. He demands blood. I don't believe in such a God, for my God is merciful to all." I want to say, "My God is full of mercy!" But don't be so blind as to believe that God is not just, and that He has no government.

Suppose Queen Victoria didn't like any man to be deprived of his liberty, and she threw all her prisons open and was so merciful that she could not bear any one to suffer for guilt. How long would she hold the scepter? How long would she rule this empire? Not twenty-four hours. Those very men who cry out about God being merciful would say: "We don't want such a Queen."

GOD IS MERCIFUL BUT JUST

God is merciful, but He will not take an unredeemed sinner into heaven. If He did, the redeemed would plant the banner of indignant objection around the throne, and heaven would revolt. God said to Adam, "On the day you sin you will surely die." Sin entered and brought death into the world. God's word must be kept. I must either die or get somebody to die for me, and in the fulness of time Christ comes forward to die for the sinner. He was without sin, but if He had committed one sin, He would have had to die for His own sin.

The life of the flesh is in the blood, but it is not blood He demands, really. It is life, and life has been forfeited. We have sinned, and death must come, or justice must take its course. Glory to God in the highest because He sent His Son, born of a woman, to take our nature and die in our stead, tasting death for every man. You take this blood out of this body of mine, and life is gone.

God demands blood. He demands life. Man has sinned, and therefore life must be forfeited, and I must die, or find somebody to die for me. My friends, I have only just touched this subject. If you read your Bibles carefully you will find the scarlet thread running through the Bible. It commenced in Eden and flows on to Revelation. I cannot find anything to tell me the way to heaven is anything but the blood.

The Bible wouldn't be worth carrying home if you take the scarlet thread out of it, and it doesn't teach anything else, for the blood commences in Genesis and goes through Revelation. That is what this book is written for. It tells its own story, and if a man should come and preach another gospel, don't believe him. If an angel should come and preach anything else, don't believe it. Don't trifle with the subject of the blood. In your dying hour you would give more to be sheltered behind this blood than for all the world.

A MOTHER'S LOVE

In the time of the California gold fever, a man went to the diggings and left his wife to follow him some time afterward. While on her voyage with her little boy, the vessel caught fire, and as there was a powder-magazine on board, the captain knew when the flames reached it the ship would be blown up. The fire could not be controlled and they took to the lifeboats, but there was not room for all. As the last boat pushed off, the mother and boy stood on the deck. One of the sailors said there was room for another. What did the mother do? She decided to perish herself in order to save her boy. She dropped him into the boat, and with a mother's last look, said: "If you should live to see your father, tell him that I died in your place."

Do you think when that boy grew up he could fail to love the mother who died to save him? This is a faint type of what Christ has done for you and me. He died for our sins. He left heaven for that purpose. Will you go away saying, "I see no beauty in Him"? May God break every heart. You will need Him when you come to cross the Jordan. You will need Him when you go up to the bar of God, and God forbid that when death comes it should find you without Christ, without God and without hope!

Not only is the vitally important subject of the blood of Christ referred to frequently in the Old Testament, but likewise in many places in the New Testament.

Let us turn to the second chapter of the Acts of the Apostles: *Him, being delivered by the determinate counsel and foreknowledge of God, ye have taken, and by wicked hands have crucified and slain* (Acts 2:23). What is this but shedding the blood of Christ, the death of Christ? Read also Acts 4:10; 5:28; 7:52; 8:32; 10:39; 17:3; 18:21; Hebrews 9:22; 1 Peter 1:19. You will find many other passages if you search for the word *blood* in a concordance.

THE MEANING OF REDEMPTION

A friend of mine was in Ireland and saw a little Irish boy who had caught a sparrow. The poor little bird was trembling and panting in his hand. The gentleman told the boy to let it go, as the bird could not do him any good, but the boy said he would not let it escape because he had been chasing it for three hours before he could catch it. The gentleman offered to buy the bird, paid the price the boy agreed to, and then took the poor bird and held it out on his palm, where it sat for a time, scarcely able to believe that it was free. At last it flew away, chirping, as if to say to the gentleman, "You have redeemed me."

That is what is meant by redemption. Satan is stronger than any man on earth, and there is no match for him but Christ. The lion of Calvary – the lion of the tribe of Judah – is stronger than the lion of hell. When Christ on Calvary said, "It is finished!" it was the shout of the conqueror.

Once, when I was revisiting my native village, I was going to a neighboring town to preach and saw a young man coming from a house in a carriage, in which was seated an old woman. I asked my companion who they were. I was told to look at the adjoining meadow and pasture, the great barns and the good house that were on the farm.

"Well," said my companion, "that young man's father drank that all up and left his wife in the poorhouse. The young man went away and worked until he had enough money to redeem that farm. Now it is his own, and he is taking his mother to church."

That is another illustration of redemption.

In the first Adam, we have lost all, but the second Adam has redeemed everything by His death. A friend of mine who was in Paris went to a great meeting of Jews, at which one of the leading men presided, and that man said the Jews had the honor of killing the Christian's God; and those Jews stamped and applauded at the statement. They were proud of the act, and cried out, "His blood be upon us, and upon our children," and that imprecation has been literally fulfilled in their history. Christ's blood either cries for our peace and salvation or for our condemnation.

BRINGING PEACE OUT OF THE BLOOD

In Colossians 1:20, the apostle Paul says, *Having made peace through the blood of the cross, by Him to reconcile all things to Himself; by Him, I say, whether they be things in earth, or things in heaven.* That is what the blood of the cross does – it brings peace. In Romans 5 it says, *Therefore being justified by faith, we have peace with God through our Lord Jesus Christ; by whom also we have access by faith into this grace wherein we stand, and rejoice in hope of the glory of God* (Romans 5:1-2). Three things are stated here: There is justification for the past as well as peace; as the believer looks back to Calvary, the blood speaks peace and pardon for guilt; and there is grace for the present and glory for the future.

John 19:34 says, *But one of the soldiers with a spear pierced His side, and forthwith came thereout blood and water.* A striking fact is revealed in this verse. The spear that went into the side of the Son of God was the crowning act of sin, the culminating crime of earth and hell. I don't see how they could have done a more cruel thing than that. What act could have been more black and hellish?

The blood came out and covered the spear, and a fountain was thus opened in the house of David for sin. The blood touched the Roman spear, and it was not long before the Roman government became at least nominally Christian. The blood ran down from His side upon the earth, and this earth has been redeemed by Him, for He will have the world by and by. He is the true Sovereign, and He will before long cast out the prince of darkness and wave His scepter from end to end of this earth. He will personally return and set up His millennial kingdom and reign over this earth. He has redeemed the earth by His blood, and He will have all He has redeemed.

THE BLOOD BRINGS ONENESS IN CHRIST

Has the blood touched you? The blood of Christ makes us one and brings us into the family of God. It enables us to cry, "Abba, Father." At the time of the American war, during the days of slavery in America, when there was much political strife and strong prejudice against black men, especially by Irishmen, I heard a preacher say that when he came to the cross for salvation he seemed to find a poor black man on one side and an Irishman on the other side, and the blood trickled down upon them and made them one. There may be strife in the world, but Christ has made one family of those he has redeemed. We are blood relatives.

When I go before an audience, there is hardly a person I have seen before but as I begin to talk about the King their eyes light up, and I see they are kinsmen, they are blood relatives, and in a short time I become attached to them. A man may go into a town a perfect stranger but as soon as he finds those who love God, they will be one. I wish Christians had more of this oneness. I hope the time will soon come when sectarian walls will be broken down, and people will not want to ask whether you belong to the Church of England, Wesleyan, or Baptist Churches. If washed in the blood, we are blood relatives.

I believe God will judge the world by the blood. "What have you done with that blood?" will be the great question in that day. If we make light of it, and send back an insulting message, saying we don't need it, we shall stand speechless before God's tribunal. If we make light of that blood, what is going to become of our souls?

JUSTIFICATION BY BLOOD

The only way a man can be brought within the family of God is by the blood. As it says in Romans 3:24, *Being justified freely by His grace through the redemption that is in Christ Jesus,* and again in Romans 5:9, *Much more then, being now justified by His blood, we shall be saved from wrath through Him.* We will be justified in all the ways in which we could not be justified by the law of Moses. When God looks into His ledger, there is nothing found against the man who is washed in the blood. One plunge in the crimson fountain, and the sinner is justified in the sight of God.

Christ was raised from the grave to justify all who put their trust in Him, and they are not only pardoned but justified as well. Justification is more than pardon. It is said of an emperor of Russia that he once sent for two noblemen who were charged with some conspiracy. One he found perfectly innocent and sent him home justified, but the other was proved guilty but was pardoned. They both returned home, but ever afterwards would stand very differently in the estimation of their emperor and neighbors. This is the difference between pardon and justification.

HAVE CONFIDENCE IN THE BLOOD

When a man is justified, he can go through the world with his head erect. Satan may come to him, and say, "You are a sinner," but the reply would be, "I know, but God has forgiven me through Christ." Revelation 1 says, *And from Jesus Christ, who is the faithful witness, and the first begotten of the dead, and the prince of the kings of the earth. Unto Him that loved us, and washed us in His own blood, and hath made us kings and priests unto God and his Father; to Him be glory and dominion for ever and ever* (Revelation 1:5-6).

Many people who try to come to Christ think they cannot approach Him unless they first become good. But He loves all Christians even before their sins are washed away. He loves them and then washes them in His own blood. It is wonderful love! To think that He loves them first and then washes them in His blood from their sins! There is no devil in hell that can pluck them out of His hand. Having been washed in the blood of the Lamb, they are perfectly safe.

THERE IS NO REMISSION WITHOUT BLOOD

It is said in Hebrews 9:22, *And almost all things are by the law purged with blood; and without shedding of blood is no remission.* It is utterly impossible that a man who makes light of the blood can be saved. There is no other name under heaven whereby we can be saved than the name of Christ Jesus. Are we willing to receive what Christ has already done? The salvation of those who trust in Him was already worked out when He said upon the cross, "It is finished."

In Matthew 26:28 we get the words of Christ Himself: *For this is my blood of the new testament, which was shed for many for the remission of sins.* That was what Christ Himself said about the blood. He could have saved His life, but He loved the human family so much that He shed His blood to redeem them. He opened the fountain referred to in these lines from the hymn "There Is a Fountain":

"There is a fountain filled with blood,
Drawn from Emmanuel's veins."

That hymn will last as long as the Church, and so will others such as "Rock of Ages":

> "Rock of ages, cleft for me,
>   Let me hide myself in Thee."

There is a great deal about the blood in these hymns, and they will all live. Every hymn into which the scarlet thread is woven will live. There is another sweet hymn, "Just as I Am," that will last through all ages:

> "Just as I am, without one plea
>   But that Thy blood was shed for me."

In Hebrews 10:19-20, we read, *Having therefore, brethren, boldness to enter into the holiest by the blood of Jesus, by a new and living way, which He hath consecrated for us, through the veil, that is to say, his flesh.* When Christ's work was done, the veil of the temple was rent from top to bottom. God came out of the holy of holies, and man can now go in. In this dispensation, He makes kings and priests of all His people. Everyone can come right into the presence of God Himself.

In the Jewish dispensation, none but the high priests could enter into the holy of holies, but the veil being rent, God came out and man can go in through the veil of His flesh. *Let us draw near with a true heart in full assurance of faith, having our hearts sprinkled from an evil conscience, and our bodies washed with pure water* (Hebrews 10:22).

Let us hold fast the profession of our faith. The new and living way has been opened by His blood. The only thing that Christ left down here was His blood. When He ascended to heaven, He took with Him His flesh and bones, but His shed blood was left on this earth.

THE BLOOD IS AN EITHER/OR CHOICE

The blood cries either for my damnation or for my salvation. If I make light of the blood, and trample it under my feet, then it cries out for condemnation. But if I am sheltered by the blood, there is no condemnation for me. God dealt in judgment with Cain, and when Pilate wanted to know what to do with Christ, he washed his hands and declared that He was innocent. The assembled mob said, "Let His blood be upon us and our children, not to save us, but to condemn us." Would that they had said, "Let His blood be upon us to save us and protect us."

Nearly 1900 years have rolled away, and the Jews are wanderers on the face of the earth without a king. Their having been scattered all these years, what a proof it is the word of God is true! May our prayer be, "His blood be upon us and our children, not to condemn us, but to save us." Let that be our prayer, that we may know what it is to be sheltered by the blood of God's dear Son. The blood of the cross speaks peace. If I am sheltered, there is peace, but there is no peace until my sin is covered. If you committed sin against a man, you would get no peace until that was forgiven. Men are running after peace, and if it could be bought in the market, many would give hundreds of thousands of pounds to secure it. The blood of Christ speaks peace, and it will bring peace to every guilty conscience and aching heart today if you only seek it.

In Hebrews 10:28-29, we read: *He that despised Moses' law died without mercy under two or three witnesses: of how much sorer punishment, suppose ye, shall he be thought worthy, who hath trodden underfoot the Son of God, and hath counted the blood of the covenant, wherewith he was sanctified, an unholy thing, and hath done despite unto the Spirit of grace?* To me these are very solemn verses. I don't see how anyone can sit here and hear these verses read and be content to remain unsaved.

"They died without mercy," but how much more dire will be the punishment of those who live in this age with an open Bible, which tells how Christ died to redeem us?

In Revelation 12:11, Scripture says: *And they overcame him by the blood of the Lamb, and by the word of their testimony; and they loved not their lives unto the death.* They overcame by the blood. I don't believe there is a word in the Bible Satan fears more than the word "blood." Judging from past experience, I shall probably receive many letters tomorrow attacking me for what I have said today. These letters will say it is heathenish to stand up and preach what would only do for an unenlightened age. May God forgive those who dare to say such things. If you will read your Bible in the light of Calvary, you will find there is no other way of coming to heaven but by the blood. The devil does not fear ten thousand preachers who preach a bloodless religion.

A man who preaches a bloodless religion is doing the devil's work, and I don't care who he is.

THE BLOOD BRINGS VICTORY

It is said of old Dr. Alexander, of Princeton Seminary, that when he parted with the students who were going to preach the gospel, he would take them by the hand, and say, "Young man, make much of the blood. Make much of the blood."

As I have travelled up and down Christendom, I have found out that a minister who gives a clear depiction of this doctrine is successful. A man who covers up the cross, though he may be an intellectual man and draw large crowds, cannot touch the heart and conscience. There will be no life there, and his church will be like a gilded sepulchre. God honors those men who preach the doctrine of the cross, who hold up Christ as the sinner's only hope of heaven and only substitute, and who make much of the blood. Souls are always saved where that truth is preached.

I would say, "Make much of the blood." May God help us to make much of the blood of His Son. It cost God so much to give it to us. Shall we try to keep it from the world, which is perishing for the want of it? The world can get along without us but not without Christ. Let us preach Christ in season and out of season. Let us go to the sick and dying and hold up the Savior who came to seek and save them, and who died to redeem them.

CHRIST WILL CONQUER

A story of Julian the Apostate, in Rome, says that when he was trying to stamp out Christianity he was pierced in the side by an arrow. He pulled the arrow out, and taking a handful of blood as it flowed from the wound, threw it into the air, shouting, "You Galilean, have you conquered?" Yes, this Galilean is going to conquer. May God help us to allow no uncertainty on this doctrine.

I would rather give up my life than give up this doctrine. Take that away, and what is my hope in heaven? Am I to depend upon my works? They are worthless when it comes to the question of salvation. I must get salvation distinct and separate from works, for it is "to him that worketh not," but believes in Christ. None will walk the celestial pavement of heaven but those who are washed in the blood. The first man that went up from this earth was probably Abel. You can see Abel putting his little lamb upon the altar, thus placing blood between him and his sin. Abel sang a song the angels could not join in. There must have been one song of redemption in heaven, because Abel had no one to join him. But there is a great chorus now, for the redeemed have been going up for six thousand years, and they sing of Him who is worthy to receive honor because He died to save us from condemnation.

ROBES MADE WHITE THROUGH THE BLOOD

In Revelation 7:14 we read, *And I said unto him, Sir, thou knowest. And he said to me, "These are they which came out of great tribulation, and have washed their robes, and made them white in the blood of the Lamb."* Sinner, how are you going to get your robes clean if you don't get them washed in the blood of the Lamb? How are you going to wash them? Can you yourself make them clean? Oh, may we all reach that paradise above! There they are singing the sweet song of redemption, and may it be the happy lot of each of us to join them. It may be only a short time, at the longest, before we shall be there and shout the song of redemption and sing the sweet song of Moses and the Lamb.

There, *They shall hunger no more, neither thirst anymore; neither shall the sun light on them, nor any heat. For the Lamb which is in the midst of the throne shall feed them, and lead them unto living fountains of water: and God shall wipe all tears from their eyes* (Revelation 7:16-17).

On that day, skeptics and scoffers will pray for the rocks and mountains to fall and cover them from the wrath of God. If you die without Christ, without hope, and without God, where will you be? Sinner, be wise! Don't make light of the blood!

BLOOD AND THE DYING SAINT

An aged minister of the gospel, when dying, said, "Bring me the Bible." Putting his finger upon the verse that says, "The blood of Jesus Christ cleanses us from all sin," he said, "I die in the hope of this verse." He did not rely on his fifty years of preaching, nor his long life in the Lord's service. He relied on the blood of Christ. When we stand before God's tribunal, we shall be pure, even as He is pure, if we are washed in the blood of the Lamb.

THE PRECIOUS BLOOD

During the American war, a doctor heard a man saying, "Blood, blood, blood!" The doctor thought this was because he had seen so much blood shed upon battlefields, and he tried to soothe his mind. The man smiled, and said, "I wasn't thinking of the blood on the battlefield, but I was thinking how precious the blood of Christ is to me as I am dying." As he died his lips quivered, "Blood, blood, blood!" and he was gone.

The blood will indeed be precious when we come to our dying bed! It will then be worth more to us than all the world! One sin is enough to exclude us from heaven, but one drop of Christ's blood is sufficient to cover all our sins. Beware how you treat the gospel message of redemption through the blood.

THE SLIPPERY SLOPE

A stage driver lying on his death bed on the Pacific coast, as I was told when I was there about three years ago, kept moving one of his feet up and down, saying, "I am on the downhill grade, and cannot reach the brake." As they told me of it, I thought how many were on the down grade and could not reach the brake and were dying without God and without hope. I plead with you as a fellow traveler: Don't go out without saying, "Heaven is my home, and God is my Father." Don't let the scoffers laugh you into hell. They cannot laugh you out of it.

The blood is on the mercy seat, and while it is, you can enter into the kingdom. God says, "There is the blood. It is all I have to give. As long as it is there, you have hope. I am satisfied with the finished work of my Son. Will you be satisfied?"

Claim this as yours. How dark and sad it is to go to the death bed of an unbeliever or an atheist, or one who is dying without the light of the resurrection morning. But if we trust to Christ, death has lost its sting and the grave its victory.

An eminent minister in America, Alfred Cookman, the Robert M'Cheyne of his day, was dying, and when his friends were gathered round his couch, waiting to see him depart to be with Christ, his face lit up and with a shout of triumph he said, "I am sweeping through the gates, washed in the blood of the Lamb!" And this echoes and re-echoes through America today: "I am sweeping through the gates, washed in the blood of the Lamb!" May these be our last words, and may an abundant entrance be granted us into the gates of the heavenly city!

FROM THE HYMN "SWEEPING THROUGH THE GATES"

Who, who are these, beside the chilly wave

Just on the borders of the silent grave;
Shouting Jesus power to save,
Washed in the blood of the Lamb.

Sweeping through the gates of the new Jerusalem
Washed in the blood of the Lamb.

CHAPTER 4

CHRIST IS OUR ALL IN ALL

Where there is neither Greek nor Jew, circumcision nor uncircumcision, Barbarian, Scythian, bond nor free: but Christ is all, and in all.
– Colossians 3:11

Christ is all in all to everyone who has truly found Him. He is our Savior, Redeemer, Deliverer, Shepherd, and Teacher and also fills for us many roles, to which I desire to direct your attention.

ONE: HE IS OUR SAVIOR

In Luke 2:10-11, Christ is announced as our Savior: *Behold, I bring you good tidings of great joy, which shall be to all people. For unto you is born this day in the city of David a Saviour, which is Christ the Lord.* We learn to know Christ as our Savior, to meet Him on Mount Calvary, to look on Him as the bleeding Lamb of God, before we know Him as our Redeemer, Deliverer, and Shepherd. Now I do not know the hearts of the people and cannot know whether you can say that Christ is your Savior. There are many, I trust, who can say this, and who rejoice in His salvation. However, without being uncharitable, I am afraid there are many who know nothing personally of Jesus as their Savior.

He is offered to every one of you today as a Savior. God gave Him up freely that we all might be saved through Him. If you belong to this world, I can prove that you have a Savior. If you belonged to some other planet, then I could not say a Savior was offered to you. It is not revealed whether the people of distant worlds, if they are inhabited, require salvation or not. But this I know, that every man on this globe has a Savior offered to him.

Salvation is free to all, and I have no sympathy with those men who try to limit God's salvation to a certain few. I believe that Christ died for all who will come. I have received many letters finding fault with me, saying surely I don't believe in the doctrine of election. I do believe in election, but I have no business to preach that doctrine to the world at large. The world has nothing to do with election. It has only to do with the invitation, "Whoever wants to drink from the water of life, let him drink freely." That is the message for the sinner. I am sent to preach the gospel to all.

After you have received salvation, we can talk about election, which is a doctrine for Christians, for the Church, not for the unconverted world. Our message is "good news of great joy, for all people, for today is born a Savior, which is Christ the Lord." This Savior is offered to all people – to you. Accept Him, and God will accept you. Reject Him, and God will reject you. Your eternal destiny depends on your refusal or otherwise to accept the offered Savior. The case is simply one of giving and taking. God gives, I receive. We must, first of all, know Christ as our Savior.

TWO: HE IS OUR REDEEMER

Suppose I saw a man tumble into a river, and I were to jump in and rescue him, I should be a savior to him – I would have saved him. When I brought the man ashore, I would probably leave him and do nothing further.

But the Lord does more. He not only saves us, He redeems us – that is, buys us back. He ransoms us from the power of sin, as if I should promise to watch over that rescued man forever and see that he did not again fall into the water. The Lord not only saves us from spiritual death, but He redeems us such that, forever, death can never touch us.

He also proclaims liberty to captives.

When I was at Richmond, in the United States, black people were going to have a meeting. It was the first day of their freedom. I went to the African church, and never before or since have I heard such bursts of native eloquence.

"Mothers," said one, "rejoice today. Your little child has been sold from you for the last time. Your posterity is forever free. Glory to God in the highest! Young men, you have heard the driver's whip for the last time. You are free today! Young maidens, you have been put up on the auction-block for the last time!"

They spoke right out, they shouted for joy. Their prayers had been answered, and it was the gospel to them. In like manner, Jesus Christ proclaims liberty to the captives. Some have accepted it and some, like the poor black people, scarcely believe the good tidings, but it is nonetheless true. Christ has come to redeem us from the slavery of sin.

Now, who will accept that redemption? There was one black woman, a servant in an inn in the Southern States, who could not believe she was free.

"Be's I free or be I not?" she asked of a visitor.

Her master told her she was not, her black brethren told her she was. For two years she had been free without knowing it. She represents a great many in the Church of God today. They can have liberty, and yet they don't know it.

THREE: CHRIST IS OUR DELIVERER

The children of Israel were not only saved and redeemed from the bondage of the Egyptians, they were also delivered so that they could not be led back into bondage. Many are afraid. Because they think they are not able to hold on, they therefore shrink from making a profession. But Christ is able to keep you from falling. He is able to deliver you in the dark hour of trial and temptation from every evil device of Satan and from the snare of the fowler.

In Isaiah 49:24-25, we read: *Shall the prey be taken from the mighty, or the lawful captive delivered? But thus saith the Lord, Even the captives of the mighty shall be taken away, and the prey of the terrible shall be delivered: for I will contend with him that contendeth with thee, and I will save thy children.*

The children of Israel were saved from the cruel bondage of Egypt and were led out of the land of Goshen, but still they were not fully delivered. The great host of the Egyptians was thundering behind them. It was not till they had passed safely through the Red Sea, which, closing behind them, swallowed up the host of the enemy. It was not till then that they were free, that they were delivered.

Similarly, in our times of danger, we shall find it to be true of Christ that He delivered my soul, and again in Job 33:24-26, *Then He is gracious unto him, and saith, Deliver him from going down to the pit: I have found a ransom. His flesh shall be fresher than a child's: he shall return to the days of his youth: He shall pray unto God, and He will be favourable unto him: and he shall see His face with joy: for He will render unto man His righteousness.* And then in verse 28, *He will deliver his soul from going into the pit, and his life shall see the light.*

Here we have the saving, the redeeming, and the deliverance from the pit. Man has fallen into the deep pit, and he is kept there a lawful captive by one who is mighty. If he is to be brought back from the darkness of the pit to see the light, then we must have a ransom. God comes forward and says, "I have found a ransom." Christ is the ransom, and He will deliver us. Sound out the cry, "Christ is our deliverer." He is mighty to save. He is able to deliver.

FOUR: HE IS A LEADER

But we need something more. Look back again to the children of Israel. When they had marched gloriously through the Red Sea, they had been saved, redeemed, and delivered. Was that all they required? No. They had been brought into the wilderness. What now do they need? They have to go into the pathless desert. They require a leader, and Christ is the way and the leader. Are we in difficulties, in doubt, or in perplexity? Christ is our way. *I am the way, the truth, and the life* (John 14:6).

Some say, "If I am converted and become religious, I don't know what church I would go to. There are so many different churches and denominations. I really don't know which is the right one." To people who are bewildered and do not know which is the true way, I would say, "Look only to Him who says, 'I am the way.'"

He is the only true way, and if you want to reach the kingdom you have only to follow Him. We may be in darkness, but He is able to lead us in the right path. He is the Shepherd of His flock. He will go before us and lead us. He is calling upon us to rise and follow Him, and He will lead us by a way we do not know. He will guide us to the green pastures if we only look to Him.

All that the children of Israel had to do was to follow the pillar of cloud. If the cloud rested, they rested. If the cloud moved forward, then they moved. I can imagine that the first thing Moses did, when the gray dawn of morning broke, was to look up and see if the cloud was still over them. By night it was a pillar of fire, lighting up the camp and filling them with a sense of God's protecting care. By day, it was a cloud shielding them from the fierce heat of the sun's rays and sheltering them from the sight of their enemies.

Israel's Shepherd could lead them through the pathless desert. Why? Because He made it. He knew every grain of sand in it. They could not have a better leader through the wilderness than its Creator.

And, sinner, can you, in all your difficulties or doubts and fears, have a better leader than Jehovah? Oh, I do like that good old hymn:

> "Guide me, O Thou great Jehovah
>   Pilgrim through this barren land;
> I am weak, but Thou art mighty,
>   Hold me with Thy powerful hand. Bread of heaven,
> Feed me till I want no more."

That is the true prayer of the bewildered sinner. God is able and He is willing to lead us and to feed us. Nehemiah 9:15 tells us that God gave them bread from heaven for their hunger, and brought water out of the rock for their thirst. He is still as able to lead any of us as He was four thousand years ago to lead the children of Israel, "For I am the Lord; I do not change." To every one of us He says, "Fear not, I will lead you. I will help you." Wonderful thing, is it not, to have God to help us on our way?

In our Western countries, when men go out hunting into the dense backwoods where there are no roads or paths of any kind, they take their hatchet and cut a little chip out of the bark of the trees as they go along, and then they easily find their way by these blazes. They call it "blazing the way." And so, if you will allow me the expression, Christ has "blazed the way." He has travelled the road Himself and, knowing the way, He tells us to follow Him, and He will lead us safely on high.

FIVE: HE IS OUR LIGHT

We have seen Christ is our Savior, Redeemer, Deliverer, Leader, or Way. But He is more than all that. He is our Light. "I am the light of the world," he says in John, "and he who follows me will not walk in darkness but will have the light of life." He shall have the very "light of life." It is the privilege of every Christian to walk in an unclouded sky.

But do we walk in an unclouded sky? No, most Christians are often in darkness. If I were to ask this congregation if they were all walking in the light, I believe there is scarcely one, if he spoke the true feeling of his heart, but would reply, "No, I am often in darkness." Why is that? It is because we are not following Christ and keeping close to Him. We are much in darkness when we might be in the light.

Suppose the windows of this building were all closed, and we were complaining of the darkness. What would anyone say to us? They would say, "Let in the light. Open the windows, and you'll soon have plenty of light." Similarly we must let in Christ, who is the light, and open our minds to receive Him, and we shall soon walk in light. There is a great deal of darkness at the present time, even in the hearts of God's own people. But follow Him, and you will have plenty of light. Christ will show to each of us that He is the Light, and He will do more. He will set us on fire with His light so that we also may shine as lights in this dark world.

May God help His own people to shine brightly, to flash out of darkness so that men will know that we have been with Jesus.

But remember, the world hates the light. Christ was the light of the world, and the world sought to extinguish it at Calvary. Now He has left His people to shine – "You are the light of the world." He has left us here to shine. He means us to be "living epistles, known and read by all men." The world is certain to watch and to read you and me. If we are inconsistent, then you may be sure the world will stumble after us.

The world finds plenty of difficulties on the way. We Christians should not add more stumbling-blocks by an un-Christlike walk. God help us to keep our lights burning clear and brilliant!

Out West, a friend of mine was walking along a street one dark night and saw a man approaching him with a lantern. As he came up close, he noticed by the bright light that the man had no eyes. He went past, but the thought struck him, "Surely that man is blind." He turned round, and said, "My friend, are you not blind?"

"Yes."

"Then what have you got the lantern for?"

"I carry the lantern that people may not stumble over me, of course," said the blind man.

Let us take a lesson from that blind man, and hold up our light, burning with the clear radiance of heaven, that men may not stumble over us.

SIX: WE ARE THE REFLECTED LIGHT

Objectors say that it's all moonshine about Christ's people being lights on the way. Well, that is exactly what we believe – we reflect the light of Christ.

Just like the moonshine, our light is borrowed. When we are living in the light of our Savior, we shine with His light, somewhat like the face of Moses, which shone after he had been on the mount with God. If we live in an atmosphere of heaven, we cannot help shining, but whenever we get downcast and weak in faith, then we are sure to lose our light.

I remember during the American war, I was in a prayer meeting. We were all very dark and gloomy. Things had been going against us for some time. At last an old man got up and said, "What is the matter with us, that we are downhearted and sad? It is simply our lack of faith."

Moses, Joshua, and David were men strong in faith. They believed, and therefore God honored them. From where does our lack of faith come? God is not dead. He is as powerful, as willing to help today as He ever was. Why, then, are we not full of faith in Him? It is dishonoring God to forget that He still has power though our armies are defeated, and all seems dark and gloomy.

We must get above the clouds. Some time ago when I was out West, I wanted to reach the summit of one of the mountains. I had been told that sunrise was very beautiful when seen from the summit. We got up to the halfway house one afternoon, where we were to rest till midnight, and then set out for the top. Soon a little party of us started with a good guide. Before long, it began to rain, and then it became a regular storm of thunder and lightning. I thought there was little use in going on, and said to the guide, "Guess we'd better turn back. We won't see anything this morning, with all these clouds."

"Oh," said the guide, "I expect we'll soon get through these clouds and get above them, and then we'll have a glorious view."

So we went on, while the thunders were rumbling right in our ears. But soon we began to get above the thunderclouds. The air was quite clear, and when the sun rose we had a splendid view of his rays as they tinged the hilltops. Then, as the glorious sunshine began to break on where we stood, we could see the dark cloud far beneath us. That's what God's people want – to get into the clear air above the stormy clouds and to climb higher up the mountain peak. There, far above the clouds and mists, you'll catch the first rays from the Sun of Righteousness.

Some of you may be in great darkness and gloom, but fear not. Climb higher, get nearer to the Master, and soon you'll catch His bright rays on your own soul, and they will sparkle back upon others.

But we must keep the lower lights burning. We must live as children of the light, not as children of the darkness. If we are dark and sorrowful, how is the world to know that we are children of peace, and joy, and gladness? Our determination must be to keep our lights burning. A few years ago at the mouth of Cleveland harbor, there were two lights, one at each side of the bay, called the upper and lower lights. To enter the harbor safely by night, vessels must sight both of these lights. These Western lakes are more dangerous sometimes than the ocean. One wild, stormy night a steamer was trying to make her way into the harbor. The captain and the pilot were anxiously watching for the lights, and by and by the pilot said, "Do you see the lower lights?"

"No," was the reply. "I fear we have passed them."

"Ah, there are the lights," said the pilot, "and from the bluff on which they stand, they must be the upper lights. We have passed the lower lights, and have lost our chance of getting into the harbor."

What was to be done? They looked back and saw the dim outline of the lower lighthouse against the sky. The lights had gone out.

"Can't you turn her head round?"

"No. The night is too wild for that. She won't answer her helm."

The storm was so fearful that they could do nothing. They

tried again to make for the harbor, but they crashed against the rocks and sank to the bottom. Very few escaped. The great majority found a watery grave. Why? Simply because the lower lights had gone out.

And with us the upper lights are all right. Christ Himself is the upper light, and we are the lower lights, and the cry to us is to keep the lower lights burning. That is what we have to do. In the place where God has put us, He expects us to shine, to be living witnesses, to be a bright and shining light. While we are here, our work is to shine for Him, and He will lead us safe to the sunlit shore of Canaan, where there is no more night.

SEVEN: HE IS OUR TEACHER

Christ is more than our Light. He is also our teacher.

What a wonderful thing to have a teacher sent from heaven. *If any man lack wisdom, let him ask of God, that giveth to all men liberally, and upbraideth not; and it shall be given him* (James 1:5).

"If any lack wisdom." I am afraid that a great many of us lack wisdom, and even the best of us at times will be confused. There are moments in the life of us all when we seem in a fix, when we just stand still, and say, "What do I do? I don't know what is the best way."

Leave it with God. He Himself will be our teacher!

Come unto me, all ye that labour and are heavy laden, and I will give you rest. Take my yoke upon you, and learn of me (Matthew 11:28-29). Here is a wonderful teacher. He has had a school for many thousands of years. He has had the best men in His school, but still there's room for another scholar. His college is not too full yet, and the teacher is the One sent from heaven. Any one – everyone – in this assembly may join this school. I will welcome you there. Are you in doubt about anything? Ask Jesus. He will tell you. If you are an anxious sinner, seek the good teacher, as Nicodemus did: "Master, we know that you are a teacher sent from God." If you seek Him this way, He will direct you. He will keep you and lead you into green pastures by the still waters.

I met a woman the other day who was as full of doubts and fancies as an unbeliever. She could not believe. Reading for some time the works of nonbelievers had thrown a dark and gloomy pall over her mind. It made me sad to see her in such a state. Some of you may be like her. I wish you would take Christ as your teacher, and then all darkness would flee away. Christ is able to teach us. See how He taught the disciples and never wearied of their learning from Him? So He will teach us if we will only listen to Him.

I remember, as I was coming out of the daily prayer meeting in one of our American cities a few years ago, a lady who said she wished to speak to me. Her voice trembled with emotion, and I saw at once that she was heavily burdened by something. She said she had long been praying for her husband, and she wanted to know if I would go to see him. She thought it might do him some good. He was a judge and one of the most eminent politicians in the state.

"I have heard of him," I said. "I am afraid I need not go. He is a determined infidel and I cannot argue with him."

"That is not what he wants," said the lady. "He has had too much argument already. Go and speak to him about his soul."

I said I would, although I was not very hopeful. I went to his house, was admitted to his room, and introduced myself as having come to speak to him about salvation.

"Then you have come on a very foolish errand," he said. "There's no use in attacking me, I tell you that. I am proof against all these things. I don't believe in them."

I saw that indeed, it was no use arguing with him, so I said,

"I'll pray for you, and I want you to promise me that when you are converted you'll let me know."

"Oh, yes. I'll let you know," he said in a tone of sarcasm. "Oh, yes, I'll let you know when I'm converted!"

I left him, but I continued to pray for him, and sometime subsequently I heard that the old judge was converted. I was again preaching in that city a while after that, and when I had done talking the judge himself came to me and said: "I promised I'd let you know when I was converted. I have come to tell you of it. Have you not heard of it?"

"Yes, but I would like to hear from you how it happened."

"Well," said the judge, "one night, sometime after you called on me, my wife had gone to the meeting, and there was no one in the house but the servants. I sat by the drawing room fire, and I began to think: 'Suppose my wife is right, that there is a heaven and a hell, and suppose she is on the right way to heaven. Where am I going?' I just dismissed the thought. But a second thought came: 'Surely He who created me is able to teach me.' Yes, I thought that is so. Then why not ask Him? I struggled against it, but at last, though I was too proud to get down on my knees, I just said, 'Father, all is dark. You who created me can teach me.'

"Somehow, the more I prayed the worse I felt. I was very sad. I did not wish my wife to come home and find me thus, so I slipped away to bed, and when she came into the room, I pretended to be asleep. She got down on her knees and prayed. I knew she was praying for me, and that for many long years she had been doing so. I felt as if I could have jumped up and knelt beside her, but no, my proud heart would not let me, so I lay still, pretending to be asleep. But I didn't sleep that night. I soon changed my prayer. It was now, 'O God, save me; take away this terrible burden.'

"I didn't believe in Christ even yet. I thought I'd go right straight to the Father Himself. But the more I prayed, I only became the more miserable. My burden grew heavier. The next morning I did not wish to see my wife, so I said I was not well and wouldn't wait for breakfast. I went to the office, and when the boy came, I sent him home for a holiday. When the clerks came, I told them they might go for the day. I closed the office doors. I wanted to be alone with God. I was almost frantic in my agony of heart. I cried to God to take away this load of sin. At last I fell on my knees, and cried, 'For Jesus Christ's sake, take away this load of sin.'

"At length I went to my wife's pastor, who had been praying with her for my conversion for years, and the same minister who had prayed with my mother before she died. As I walked down the street the verse that my mother had taught me came into my mind, 'Whatsoever things ye desire, when ye pray, believe that ye receive them, and ye shall have them.' Well, I thought, I have asked God, and here I am going to ask a man. I won't go. I believe I am a Christian. I turned and went home. I met my wife in the hall as I entered. I caught her hand, and said, 'I am a Christian now.'

"She turned quite pale. She had been praying for twenty-one years for me, and yet she could not believe the answer had come. We went into our room and knelt down by the very bedside where she had so often knelt to pray for her husband. There we erected our family altar, and for the first time our voices mingled in prayer. And I can only say that the last three months have been the happiest months ever I spent in my life."

Since then that judge has lived a consistent Christian life and all because he came to God, asking for guidance.

If there is one here today whose mind is filled with such unbelieving thoughts, go honestly to God, and He will teach you the right way through the dark wilderness of infidelity. He won't leave you in darkness or doubt. It is the devil's own work to lead men into such doubts, and well he knows if he once gets them there, he has them pretty safe. It is Satan's work to keep you in ignorance or doubt. It is God's work to teach you. The teacher is Christ. He is appointed by God for this work. God help us all to accept Him as our teacher.

EIGHT: HE IS OUR SHEPHERD

We have seen Christ as our Savior, Redeemer, Deliverer, Leader, Light, and Teacher, but we now see He is still more. He is also our shepherd.

It is a very sweet thought to me that the Lord is my Shepherd and I shall not want. There is no one here, except the babes, who does not understand the work of a shepherd. He watches over his flock, protects them from danger, feeds them, leads them into the best pastures. In fact, the Twenty-third Psalm is just a statement of the duties of a good shepherd: *The Lord is my Shepherd; I shall not want* (Psalm 23:1).

You want to be fed. Are you going to wander about seeking something to satisfy the cravings of your soul? I tell you, you never will find anything to satisfy the longings of your heart. The world cannot, and never could, satisfy a hungry soul. The Lord Jesus can. He is the true Shepherd, who seeks to restore your soul and lead you back to the paths of righteousness. Even to death will He lead you and guide you safely through its shadow to a better land.

Mother, father, will you claim Him as your Shepherd?

Young man, young woman, will you have Him as your Shepherd?

My little child, will you have Jesus as your Shepherd?

He will lead safely and softly. You can, all of you, if you will, for God gave Him up freely for us all that He might have us for His flock. He will lead us through life, down to the banks of the Jordan, and He will lead us across the dark river into His kingdom. He is a tender, loving Shepherd.

I sometimes meet people in the inquiry-room who are nourishing hard, bitter feelings against God, generally because they have been afflicted. A mother said to me the other day, "Mr. Moody, God has been unjust to me. He has come and taken away my child."

Dear afflicted mothers, has God not removed your children to a pure and happy life? You may not understand it now, but you will by and by. He wants to lead you up there too.

A friend of mine, who had been in eastern lands, told me he saw a shepherd who wanted his flock to cross a river. He went into the water himself and called them, but they would not follow him into the water. What did he do? He girded up his loins and lifted a little lamb under each arm, plunged right into the stream, and crossed it without even looking back. Whenever he lifted the lambs, the old sheep looked up into his face and began to bleat for them, but when he plunged into the water the dams plunged after him, and then the whole flock followed.

When they got to the other side he put down the lambs. They were quickly joined by their mothers, and there was a happy meeting. My friend says he noticed the pastures on the other side were much better and the fields greener, and on this account the shepherd was leading them across. Our great Shepherd of Palestine does that. That child which He has taken from the earth is but removed to green pastures of Canaan, and the Shepherd means to draw your hearts after it and teach you to "set your affections on things above." When He has taken your little Mary, Edith, or Julia, accept it as a call to look upward and beyond. You, mother, are you weeping bitter tears for your little one? Do not weep! Your child has gone to the place where there is neither weeping nor sorrow. Would you have it return? Surely never.

Christ is our Shepherd, faithful and loving. Though sickness or trouble, or even death itself, should come to our house and claim our dearest ones, still they are not lost, but only gone before. God help each one of us to have Him as our Shepherd.

I would like to take up the subject of Christ as our Justification, our Wisdom, our Righteousness, the Friend who sticks closer than a brother, but it would take a whole eternity to tell what Christ is to His people and what He does for them.

I remember when I was preaching on this subject in Scotland, after I had done, I said to a man that I was sorry I could not finish the subject for want of time.

"Finish the subject," said the Scotsman, "why, that would require all eternity, and even then it would not be complete. That will be the occupation of heaven."

NINE: HE BEARS OUR BURDENS

But let us look at Christ as the Bearer of our burdens. I love to think of Him as the Bearer of our burdens as well as the Bearer of our sins, which He carries although they are more numerous than the hairs of our heads. Great and terrible as these burdens are, God has laid them all on Jesus. O Christ, what burdens bowed Your head! Our load was laid on You.

That aspect of His burden we have already looked at in His work as Savior and Redeemer. I wish now to take up the sweet thought which has been a great comfort to me: Surely, He has borne our griefs and carried our sorrows.

Glorious, is it not, to know we have such a Savior? Can you feel that He has lifted your burden off your shoulders on to His own shoulder? Then you will feel light in heart.

On one occasion, after I had been talking this way, a woman came forward, and said, "Mr. Moody, it's all very well for you to talk like that about a light heart. But you are a young man, and if you had a heavy burden like me, you would talk differently. I could not talk in that way. My burden is too great."

I replied, "But it's not too great for Jesus."

She said, "I cannot cast it on Him."

"Why not? Surely it is not too great for Him. It is not that He is feeble, but it is because you will not leave it to Him. You're like many others. They will not leave it with Him. They go about hugging their burden and yet crying out against It. What the Lord wants is for you to leave it with Him, to let Him carry it for you. Then you will have a light heart, sorrow will flee away, and there will be no more sighing. What is your burden, my friend, that you cannot leave with Christ?"

She replied, "I have a son who is a wanderer on the face of the earth. None but God knows where he is."

"Cannot Christ find him, and bring him back?"

"I suppose He can."

"Then go and tell Jesus and ask Him to forgive you for doubting His power and willingness. You have no right to mistrust Him."

She went away much comforted, and I believe her wandering boy was ultimately restored to her!

This circumstance reminds me of a pious father and mother in our country whose eldest son had gone to Chicago. A neighbor of theirs was in the city on some business, and he met the young man reeling along the streets drunk. He thought, "How am I to tell his parents?" When he returned to his village, he called on the father and told him. It was a terrible blow to that father, but he said nothing to the mother till the little ones had all gone to rest, the servants had retired, and all was quiet in that little farm on the Western prairies. They drew up their chairs to the drawing room table, and then he told her the sad news.

"Our boy has been seen drunk on the streets of Chicago – drunk!"

That mother was sorely hurt. They did not sleep much that night but spent the hours in fervent prayers for their boy. About daybreak the mother felt an inward conviction that all would be well. She told the father that she had cast it on the Lord, had left her son with Jesus, and she felt He would save him.

One week later the young man left Chicago, made a journey of three hundred miles into the country, and when he reached his home, he walked in and said, "Mother, I've come home to ask you to pray for me."

Her prayer had reached heaven! She had cast her burden on Jesus, and He had borne it for her. He took the burden, presented her prayer sprinkled with the atoning blood and got it answered. In two days that young man returned to Chicago rejoicing in the Savior. What a wonderful thing it is to have Christ as our burden-bearer! How easy, how light do our cares become when cast upon Him!

Do you say Christ is nothing to you? If so, it is only because you won't have Him. He is to all who will accept Him a Savior from death, a Redeemer from the power of sin, a Deliverer from our enemies, a Leader through the wilderness. He is the way Himself, He is Light in the darkness, He is a Teacher to His people, He is the Shepherd of His flock, our Justification, Wisdom, Righteousness, Elder Brother, Burden-bearer. He is, in fact "Our all in all."

FROM THE HYMN "CHRIST IS ALL"

Then come to Christ; oh, come today,
The Father, Son, and Spirit say,
The Bride repeats the call,
For He will cleanse your guilty stains,
His love will soothe your weary pains,
For "Christ is All in All."

CHAPTER 5

NAAMAN THE SYRIAN

Read 2 Kings 5

I wish to call your attention to a man rather than to a text, one who was a great man in his own country and very honorable, a man the king delighted to honor, who stood high in position. He was captain of the host for the king of Syria, but he was a leper, and that blighted his whole life.

You cannot have a better type of sinner than Naaman was. I don't care who or what he is, nor what position he holds – all men alike have sinned, and all have to bear the same burden of death. All have sinned, and come short of the glory of God, and all men must stand in judgment before God. What a gloom that throws over our whole life!

But he was a leper. There was no physician to help him in Syria. None of the eminent doctors in Damascus could do him any good and neither could any in Jerusalem. There was no balm in Gilead. If he was to get rid of the leprosy, the power must come from on high. It must be someone unknown to Naaman, for he did not know God.

A LITTLE MISSIONARY POINTS THE WAY

But I will tell you what they had in Syria. They had one of God's children, and she was a little girl, a captive. Naaman knew nothing about her, though she was one of his household. He knew nothing about this little Israelite, and I can imagine her one day as she said to Mrs. Naaman, her mistress, that there was a prophet in her country who could cure her master of his leprosy.

"Would to God," the maid said, "my lord were with the prophet in Samaria! For he would cure him of his leprosy." There's faith for you!

"What are you talking about?" asks the mistress. "Did you ever hear of anybody being cured of leprosy?"

"It is true, I can assure you," said the little girl. "We have physicians down there who can cure anyone."

So at last someone told the king about what the little maid of Israel had said. Naaman stood high in the king's favor because he had recently won a great victory, and he was called a lord, perhaps a prince who stood near the throne.

The king said, "You had better go down to Samaria and see if there is anything in it, and I will give you letters of introduction to the king of Israel."

MONEY WILL NOT BUY SALVATION

He would give Naaman letters of introduction to the king, but that's just man's idea. The notion was that if anybody could help him, it was the king, and that the king had power both with God and man. Oh, my friends, it is a good deal better to know a man that knows God! A man acquainted with God has more power than any earthly potentate. Gold can't do everything.

Away goes Naaman down to Samaria with his kingly introduction, and he takes with him a lot of gold and silver. That is man's idea again. He is going to pay for a great doctor, and he took about £100,000 sterling, as far as I can make it out, to pay for the doctor's bill. There are a good many men who would willingly pay that sum if with it they could buy the favor of God and get rid of the curse of sin. If money could do it, how many would buy salvation! But thank God, it is not for sale. You must buy it at God's price, and that is without money and without human price. Naaman found that out.

My dear friends, did you ever ask yourselves which is worse, the leprosy of sin or the leprosy of the body? For my own part, I would a thousand times sooner have leprosy of the body eating out my eyes and my feet and my arms! I would rather be loathsome in the sight of my fellow men than die with the leprosy of sin in my soul and be banished from God forever! The leprosy of the body is bad, but the leprosy of sin is a thousand times worse. It has cast angels out of heaven, and it has ruined the best and strongest men that ever lived in the world. Oh, how it has pulled men down! The leprosy of the body could not do that.

But there is one thing about Naaman that I like, and that is his earnestness of purpose. He was quite willing to go one hundred and fifty miles and to take the advice of this little girl.

A good many people say, "Oh, I don't like such and such a minister. I would like to know where he comes from and what he has done and whether any bishop has laid his hands on his head."

My dear friends, never mind the minister – it is the message you want. If someone were to send me a telegraph message, and the news were important, I shouldn't stop to ask about the messenger who brought it. I should want to read the news. I should look at the message and not at the boy who brought it.

So it is with God's message. The good news is everything, the minister nothing. The Syrians looked down with contempt on the Israelites and yet this great man was willing to take the good news at the hands of this little girl and listen to the words that came from her lips. If I got lost in London, I would be willing to ask anybody which way to go, even if it were only a shoeblack boy and, in point of fact, a boy's word in such a case is often better than a man's. It is the way I want, not the person who directs me.

PRIDE BROUGHT LOW

But there was one drawback in Naaman's case. Though he was willing to take the advice of the little girl, he was not willing to take the remedy. The stumbling block of pride stood in his way. The remedy the prophet offered him was a terrible blow to his pride. I have no doubt he expected a grand reception from the king of Israel, to whom he brought letters of introduction. He had been victorious on many battlefields and held high rank in the army. Perhaps we may call him Major-General Naaman of Syria, or he might have been higher in rank even than that. Bearing with him kingly credentials, he expected no doubt a distinguished reception. But the king, when he heard of Naaman's arrival and what he wanted, instead of rushing out to meet him simply tore his mantle, and said, "Am I God, to kill and to make alive?"

But at last the king remembered Elisha the prophet, and he said, "There is a subject in my kingdom who may be able to help you and cure your leprosy."

And I can imagine Naaman's pride reasoning thus: "Surely the prophet will feel very much exalted and flattered that I, the great Syrian general, should come and call upon him," and, probably, full of those proud thoughts, he drives up to the prophet's humble dwelling with his chariot, his team of four horses and his splendid retinue. Naaman drove up in grand style to the prophet's house, and as nobody seemed to be coming out to greet him, he sent in his message: "Tell the prophet Major-General Naaman of Syria has arrived and wishes to see him."

THE PROPHET DELIVERS A MESSAGE

Elisha takes it very coolly. He does not come out to see him, but as soon as he learns his errand he sends his servant to tell him to dip seven times in the river Jordan, and he shall be clean. Now that was a terrible blow to Naaman's pride. I can imagine him saying to his servant, "What did you say? Did I understand you right? Dip seven times in the Jordan?! Why, we call the river Jordan a ditch in our country."

But the only answer he got was, "The prophet says, 'Go and dip seven times in the Jordan, and your flesh shall become like the flesh of a little child.'"

I can imagine Naaman's indignation as he asks, "Are not Abana and Pharpar, rivers of Damascus, better than all the waters of Israel? May I not wash in them, and be clean?"

So he turned and went away in a rage.

The fact was, the Jordan never had any great reputation as a river. It flowed into the Dead Sea, and that sea never had a harbor to it, and its banks were not half so beautiful as those of the rivers of Damascus. Damascus was one of the most beautiful cities in the world, and it is said that when Mahomet beheld it he turned his head aside for fear it should divert his thoughts from heaven. Naaman turned away from the Jordan in a rage.

"Here am I, a great conqueror, a successful general on the battlefield, holding the very highest rank in the army," he says, "and yet this prophet does not even come out to meet me. He simply sends a message. I thought he would surely come out to me and stand and call on the name of the Lord his God and strike his hand over the place and cure the leper."

THE FOLLY OF "I THOUGHT"

There it is. I never knew a man yet who, when talking about his sins, didn't always say, "Yes, but I thought so and so."

"Mr. Moody," they say, "I will tell you what I think. I will tell you my opinion."

In Chapter 55 of Isaiah it says, *For my thoughts are not your thoughts, neither are your ways my ways, saith the Lord* (Isaiah 55:8). And so it was with Naaman. In the first place, he thought a good big doctor's fee would do it all and settle everything up. And besides that, he thought that going to the king with his letters of introduction would do it. Those were Naaman's first thoughts.

"I thought." Exactly so. He turned away in rage and disappointment. He thought the prophet would have come out to him very humble and very subservient and bid him do some great things. Instead of that, Elisha, who was very likely busy writing, did not even come to the door or the window. He merely sent out the message, "Tell him to dip seven times in the Jordan." And away went Naaman, saying, "I thought," "I thought," "I thought."

I have heard that tale so often that I am tired of it. I will tell you just what I think about it, and what I advise you to do – give it up and take God's words, God's thoughts, God's ways. I never yet knew a man converted just in the time and manner he expected to be.

Now, there is a class of people in our country who have been looked down upon there just as they have been in yours. I mean the Methodists. And I have heard people say, "Well, if ever I am converted, it won't be in a Methodist church. You won't catch me there." I never knew a man say that but, at last, if converted at all, it was in a Methodist church. A man, to be converted, has to give up his will, his ways, and his thoughts. And I have noticed this, that when a man says, "Well, if ever I am converted, it will be in this way or that," God leads him in a quite contrary direction.

And Naaman, after his anger had abated and cooled down a little, took a second thought, which proved the best, although his pride had been so dreadfully humbled.

THE SIMPLICITY OF THE REMEDY

While Naaman was wavering in his mind and thinking on what was best to be done, one of his servants drew near and made a very sensible observation.

"My lord, if the prophet had told you to do some great thing, would you not have done it? How much better, then, when he says to you, 'Wash, and be clean?'"

There is a great deal of truth in that. If Elisha had said to him, "Go back to Syria on your hands and knees," he would most likely have done it. If he had said, "Go back all the way on one foot," he would have tried to do it. Or if Elisha had said, "Give ten thousand pieces of gold for the medicine I shall offer you, and you will be cleansed," no doubt he would have done it. But to tell him merely to dip in the river Jordan seven times, why, it seemed absurd on the face of it. And now this servant suggests to him that he had better go down to the Jordan and try the remedy, because it is a very simple solution.

I can hear Naaman, still reluctant to believe, saying, "Why, if there is such cleansing power in the waters of the Jordan, wouldn't every leper in Israel go down and dip in them and be healed?"

"Now that you have come a hundred and fifty miles," urges the servant, "don't you think you should do what he tells you? After all, you can try it, and he says clearly, my lord, that your flesh will become like that of a little child."

Naaman eventually accepts this word. His anger is cooling down, he has got over the first flush of his indignation, and he says, "I think I might as well try it."

That was the starting point of his faith, although he still

thought it a foolish thing and could not bring himself to believe that the result would be what the prophet had said. How many men have told me right to my face they did not believe a man could be saved by simply obeying God? Faith, they thought, was not enough, they must do something. They will have it that there must be a little asking and reasoning and striving and wrestling with God before they can get the blessing.

I recollect once praying with a man for his conversion, and just when I thought conviction had been brought home to him, he turned round and said, "Who do you think Melchizedek was, Mr. Moody?" And then I have had others who, when I have been praying with them that their sins might be taken away, would turn round and ask me, "Do you believe in infant baptism, Mr. Moody?" My friends, you need not trouble yourselves about those questions, but, if you wish to be saved, just do as the Bible tells you. *And they said, Believe on the Lord Jesus Christ, and thou shalt be saved, and thy house* (Acts 16:31). The salvation of God requires from the sinner unconditional surrender.

And at last Naaman's will was conquered, subdued and broken. He had faith, and he surrendered. I recollect when General Grant was besieging a town which was the stronghold of the Confederacy, some of the officers sent word that they would leave the city if he would let them go with their men. But General Grant sent word, "No, nothing but an unconditional surrender!" Then they sent word that they would go if he would let them take their flag with them. But the answer was, "No, an unconditional surrender." At last the beleaguered walls were broken down, and the city entered, and then the enemy made a complete and unconditional surrender.

So with Naaman. He got to the point where he was willing to obey, and the Scripture tells us that obedience is better than sacrifice.

NAAMAN OBEYS AND IS HEALED

Naaman goes down to the river and takes the first dip, and I can imagine him looking at himself, and saying to his servant as he comes up, "There. Here I am, no better than I was when I went in. If one-seventh of the leprosy was gone, I should be content."

Then down he goes a second time, and he comes up puffing and blowing and still as much a leper as ever, so, he goes down again and again, the third, fourth, fifth, and sixth time, with the same result, as much a leper as ever. And the people standing on the banks of the river probably said, as they certainly would in our day, "Why, that man has gone clean out of his mind."

When he comes up the sixth time, he looks at himself, and says, "Ah, no better. What a fool I have made of myself. How they will all laugh at me. I wouldn't have the generals and aristocracy of Damascus know that I have been dipping in the Jordan for all the world. However, since I have gone this far, I'll make the seventh plunge."

He has not altogether lost faith, and down he goes the seventh time and comes up again. He looks at himself, and shouts out loud for joy.

"I am well! My leprosy is all gone! All gone! My flesh has become again like that of a little child. I never knew such a thing. I never felt so happy in all my life. I thought I was a great and a happy man when I accomplished that victory, but, thank God, praise God, I am the happiest man alive!"

He comes up out of Jordan, puts on his clothes, goes back to the prophet and wants to pay him. That's just the old story. Naaman wants to give money for his cure. How many people want to do the same nowadays? It would have spoiled the story of grace if the prophet had taken anything. You may give a thank-offering to God's cause, not to purchase salvation, but because you are saved. The prophet Elisha refused to take anything, and I can imagine no one felt more joyful than he did. Naaman starts back to Damascus a very different man than he was when he left it. The dark cloud has gone from his mind, and he is no longer a leper in fear of dying from a loathsome disease. He lost the leprosy in the Jordan when he did what the man of God told him, and if you obey the voice of God, even while I am speaking to you, the burden of your sins will fall from off you, and you shall be cleansed. It is all done by the power of faith.

You may be sure that when he got home there was no small stir in Naaman's house. I can just see his wife when he gets back. She has been watching and looking out of the window for him with a great burden on her heart, and when she asks him, "Well, husband, how is it?" I can see the tears running down his cheeks as he says, "Thank God, I am well," and then they embrace each other, and pour out mutual expressions of rejoicing and gladness, and the servants are just as glad as their master and mistress, as they have been waiting eagerly for the news. There never was a happier household than Naaman's now that he is rid of leprosy.

And so, my friends, it will be with your own households if you will only get rid of the leprosy of sin today. Not only will there be joy in your own hearts and at home, but there will also be joy among the saints in heaven.

Another thought is suggested to us by this history of Naaman. The fifteenth verse of the chapter shows what Naaman's faith led him to believe. *And he returned to the man of God, he and all his company, and came, and stood before him: and he said, Behold, now I know that there is no God in all the earth, but in Israel: now therefore, I pray thee, take a blessing of thy servant* (2 Kings 5:15).

I particularly want to call your attention to the words, "I know." There is no hesitation about it, no qualifying the expression. Naaman doesn't now say, "I think." He says, "I know there is a God who has power to forgive sins and to cleanse leprosy."

Then there is another thought. Naaman left only one thing in Samaria, and that was his leprosy; and the only thing God wishes you to leave with Him is your sin, and yet it is the only thing you seem not to care about giving up.

"I love leprosy," you say. "It is so delightful, I can't give it up. I know God wants it, that He may make me clean, but I can't give it up."

What downright madness it is for you to love leprosy, and yet that is your condition.

"But," says someone, "I don't believe in sudden conversions."

Don't you? Well, how long did it take Naaman to be cured? The seventh time he went down, away went the leprosy. Read the great conversions recorded in the Bible. Saul of Tarsus, Zacchaeus, and a host of others. How long did it take the Lord to bring them around? They were affected in a minute. We are born in iniquity, shaped in it, dead in trespasses and sin, but when spiritual life comes, it comes in a moment, and we are free from both sin and death.

The other day, as I was walking down the street, I heard some people laughing and talking, and one of them said, "There will be no difference, it will be all the same a hundred years hence." And the thought flashed across my mind, "Will there be no difference?"

Where will you be a hundred years hence? Young man, just ask yourself the question, "Where will I be?" Some of you who are getting on in years may be in eternity ten years hence. Where will you be, on the left or the right hand of God? I cannot tell your feelings, but I can my own.

A hundred years from now all this vast audience will be gone. Some will probably be gone in less than a week, in less than a month or a year, and at the best we shall all be gone in a few more years. I ask you once again, "Where will you spend eternity? Where will you be a hundred years hence?"

A NOBLEMAN IS CONVERTED

I heard the other day of a man who came a few years ago from the Continent and brought letters with him to eminent physicians from the emperor. The letters said, "This man is a personal friend of mine, and we are afraid he is going to lose his reason. Do all you can for him."

The doctor asked him if he had lost any dear friends in his own country, or any position of importance, or what it was that was weighing on his mind. And the young man said, "No, but my father and grandfather and I were brought up as unbelievers, and for the last two or three years this thought has been haunting me, 'Where will I spend eternity?' And the thought of it follows me day and night."

The doctor said, "You have come to the wrong physician, but I will tell you of one who can cure you," and he told him of Christ and read to him from Chapter 53 of Isaiah, *But he was wounded for our transgressions, he was bruised for our iniquities: the chastisement of our peace was upon him; and with his stripes we are healed* (Isaiah 53:5).

The young man said, "Doctor, do you believe that?" The doctor told him he did, and the young man prayed and wrestled with his spirit, and at last the dear light of Calvary shone on his soul. A few years ago, he was writing to this same doctor as only one Christian can to another. He had settled the question in his own mind at last where he would spend eternity, and I ask you sinners to settle it before you leave this hall tonight. It is for you to decide. Shall it be with the saints, and martyrs, and prophets, or in the dark caverns of hell, amidst blackness and darkness forever? Make haste to be wise, for how will we escape if we neglect so great a salvation?

NOW IS THE TIME TO DECIDE

At our church in Chicago, I was closing the meeting one day when a young soldier got up and entreated the people to decide for Christ at once. He said he had just come from a dark scene. A comrade of his, he said, who had enlisted with him, had a father who was always entreating him to become a Christian, and in reply he always said he would when the war was over. At last he was wounded, and was put into the hospital, but got worse and was gradually sinking.

One day, a few hours before he died, a letter came from his sister, but he was too badly hurt to read it. It was such an earnest letter! The comrade read it to him, but he did not seem to understand it, he was so weak, till it came to the last sentence, which said, "Oh, my dear brother, when you get this letter, will you not accept your sister's Savior?" The dying man sprang up from his cot, and said, "What do you say? What do you say?" and then, falling back on his pillow, feebly exclaimed, "It is too late! It is too late!"

My dear friends, thank God it is not too late for you today. The Master is still calling you. Are you going to let present opportunity pass without coming to Christ? Are you going to let these solemn moments come to an end without entering the ark? Let every one of us, young and old, rich and poor, come to Christ at once, and He will put all our sins away.

FROM THE HYMN "ONLY A STEP"

Only a step to Jesus!
O why not come, and say,
"Gladly to Thee, my Savior,
I give myself away."

CHAPTER 6

ONE WORD - GOSPEL

Moreover, brethren, I declare unto you the
gospel which I preached unto you, which
also ye have received, and wherein ye stand.
– 1 Corinthians 15:1

I take for my text the one word – *gospel*. I do not think there is a word in the English language that is so little understood in this Christian land of England as this very word, *gospel*. We have heard it from our earliest childhood up. There is not a day, and with some of us not an hour during the day, but that we hear the word. And yet I say it takes a partaker of the gospel a long time before he really knows the meaning of the word. It means "good tidings." I think it would do us good sometimes to get a dictionary and hunt up the meaning of some of the words we use so often, even some of those Bible words, such as *gospel* and *Christ*. I think it would change our ideas.

I think it would be very joyful if everyone really believed that the gospel is good news. Let a man or a boy bring a message into this audience and hand it to anyone here, and if it brings good news you can see it immediately in the man's face, which lights up when he opens the message. You can see he really believes it. And if it is really good news, if it brings him the tidings of a long-lost boy coming home, if his wife is sitting next to him, he passes it to her. He wants her to have knowledge of it too. He does not wait for her to ask for it, and he does not wait till they get home. So, when I preach, if I am near enough to look into their eyes, I see the faces of those who really believe the gospel light up and they look remarkably sharp. But those who do not believe it put on a long face and look as if you had brought them a death-warrant or invited them to attend a funeral.

IT IS THE BEST NEWS

No better news ever came out of heaven than the gospel. No better news ever fell upon the ears of the family of man than the gospel. Hark the heralds! Hear the shepherds talking to one another after the angels had gone away. They believed the message, and they were full of joy. You can see them on the way to Bethlehem. They said, "Let us go and see what has taken place." And what was the message that the angels brought to those shepherds?

> Behold, I bring you good tidings of great joy, which shall be to all people. For unto you is born this day in the city of David a Saviour. (Luke 2:10-11)

If those shepherds had been like a good many people at the present time, they would have said, "We do not believe it is good news. It is all excitement. Those angels want to get up a revival. Those angels are trying to excite us. Don't you believe them."

That is what Satan is saying now. "Don't you believe the gospel is good news." He knows the moment a man believes good news, he receives it. I never saw a man in all my life that did not like good news and every man and woman that is under the power of the devil does not believe the gospel is good news. The moment you are out from under his power and influence, then you believe it. May God grant that the gospel may sink deep into your hearts and that you may believe it and be saved.

It is the best news that ever came to this sin-cursed world. We are dead in trespasses and sin, and God wants us to be reconciled. It is a gospel of reconciliation, and God is shouting from the heights of glory, "Oh, you men, I am reconciled, now be you reconciled!"

We have glorious news to tell you – God is reconciled and beseeches his subjects to be reconciled. The great apostle says, *We beseech you in Christ's stead, be ye reconciled to God* (2 Corinthians 5:20). The moment a man believes the gospel, down goes his arm of rebellion, and the unequal controversy is over. A light from Calvary crosses his path, and he can walk in unclouded sun, if he will. It is the privilege of every man and woman from this hour to walk in unclouded sun – if they will. What has brought darkness into the world? Darkness came because of sin, and the man who does not believe the gospel is blinded by the god of this world.

I want to tell you why I like the gospel. It is because it has been the very best news I have ever heard. That is the reason I like to preach it, because it has done me so much good. I do not think a man can preach the gospel until he believes it himself. A man must know it down deep in his own heart before he can tell it out, and then he tells it out very poorly at the best.

We are very poor ambassadors and messengers, but never mind the messenger, take hold of the message. If a boy brought me good news tonight, I would not care about the look of the boy. I would not care whether he was black or white, learned or unlearned. The message is what would do me good. A great many look at the messenger instead of the message, but never mind the messenger. My friends, get hold of the message tonight. The gospel is what saves, and what I want is that you may believe the gospel now.

CHRIST DIED FOR OUR SINS

Paul says in this fifteenth chapter of First Corinthians what the gospel is. He says, *I declare to you the gospel* (1 Corinthians 15:1). And the first thing he states in the declaration to these Corinthians is this: *Christ died for our sins according to the Scriptures* (1 Corinthians 15:3). That was the old-fashioned gospel. I hope we never get away from it. I don't want anything but that old, old story. Some people have ears itching for something new, but bear in mind there is no new gospel. Christ died for our sins. If He did not, how are we going to get rid of them? Would you insult the Almighty by offering the fruits of this frail body to atone for sin? If Christ did not die for our sins, what is going to become of our souls?

And then Paul goes on to tell us that Christ was buried and that Christ rose again.

Christ is risen, and He burst apart the bands of death. Death could not hold Him. I can imagine, when they laid Him in Joseph's sepulchre, if our eyes could have been there, we would have seen death sitting over that grave, saying, "I have Him; He is my victim. He said He was the resurrection and the life. Now I have hold of Him in my cold embrace. Look at Him. There He is. He has had to pay tribute to me. Some thought He was never going to die. Some thought I would not get Him. But He is mine."

But look again. The glorious morning comes, and the Son of man sundered the bands of death and came out of the tomb. We do not worship a dead God but a Savior who still lives. Yes,

He rose from the grave, and they saw Him ascend. That is what Paul calls the gospel, not only Christ's death and burial but His ascension into heaven. He went up and took His seat at the right hand of God, and He will come back again.

The gospel consists of five things: Christ's death, burial, resurrection, ascension, and coming again, for he said, *I will come again* (John 14:3). Thanks be to God, He is coming back by and by. He will come and take the kingdom. He will wave His scepter from the rivers to the ends of the earth. A little while and He shall rule and reign. Let us lift up our heads and rejoice that the time of our redemption draws near.

And let us get back to the simple gospel. Christ died for our sins. We must know Christ at Calvary first, as our substitute, as our Redeemer, and the moment we accept Him as our Savior and our Redeemer, then we become partakers of the gospel. The moment I believe on the Lord Jesus Christ as my substitute, as my Savior, that moment I get light and peace.

I know some people say, "It is not Christ's death, it is Christ's life. Do not be preaching so much about the death of Christ, preach about His life."

My friends, that never will save anyone. Paul says, "I declare unto you the gospel. Christ died" – not Christ lived – Christ died for our sins, and in His own body bore our sins on the tree. Because of that, when I accept of Christ as my Savior, as my substitute, then I am justified for all the things for which I could not be justified by the law of Moses.

The reason I like the gospel is that it has taken out of my path the worst enemies I ever had. My mind rolls back twenty years to before I was converted, and I think very often how dark it used to seem at times as I thought of the future. There was death. What a terrible enemy it seemed! I was brought up in a little village in New England. It was the custom there when a person was buried to toll out the age of the man at his funeral.

I used to count the strokes of the bell. Death never entered that village and tore away one of the inhabitants but that I always used to count the tolling of the bell. Sometimes it would be up to seventy, or between seventy and eighty, beyond the life allotted to man, when man seemed to be living on borrowed time. Sometimes it would be clear down in the teens, and childhood, and death would take away one of my own age.

It made a solemn impression on me, because I used to be a great coward. When it comes to death, some men say, "I do not fear it." I feared it and felt terribly afraid when I thought of the cold hand of death feeling for the cords of life and being launched out to eternity, to an unknown world. I used to have terrible thoughts about God, but they are all gone now. Death has lost its sting, and as I go through the world I can shout now, when the bell is tolling, *O death, where is thy sting?* (1 Corinthians 15:55) and I hear a voice rolling down from Calvary, "Buried in the bosom of the Son of God." He robbed death of its sting. He took the sting of death into His own bosom.

If you take a wasp and take the sting out of that wasp, you will not be any more afraid of it than you would of a little fly. The sting has been taken out. And you need not be afraid of death if you are in Christ. Christ died for your sin. The penalty, the wages of sin is death. Christ received the wages on Calvary, and therefore there is no condemnation. All that death can get now is this old Adam. I do not care how quickly I get rid of it. I will get a better body, a resurrected body, a glorified body, a body much better than this.

Yes, my friends, *To die* [says the apostle] *is gain* (Philippians 1:21).

WITHOUT CHRIST, DEATH IS FEARED

If a man is in Christ, let death come. Suppose death should come stealing up into this pulpit and lay his cold, icy hand upon my heart, and it should cease to throb. I would rise to another world and be present with the King. I would be absent from the body but present with the Lord. That is not bad news.

There is no use in trying to conceal it: Death is an enemy to a man's rest. How glorious it is to think that when you die you will sink into the arms of Jesus, and He will carry you away to a world of light. A little while longer here, a few more tears, and then you can gain an unbroken rest in that world of light. The gospel turns that enemy into a friend, and you even shout for death.

I used to go and look into the cold, silent grave, and I used to think of that terrible hour when I would have to be laid down in it, and this body would be eaten up by the worm. But now the grave has lost its terror and gloom, and I can look down into the grave and shout over it, and cry out, *O grave, where is thy victory?* (1 Corinthians 15:55). I hear a shout coming up from the grave, the shout of the Conqueror, of Him who has been down and measured the depth of it, of my Lord and Savior: "Because I live, you shall also live." Yes, the grave has lost its victory. The grave has no terror to the man in Christ Jesus. The gospel takes that enemy out of the way.

SIN IS PUT AWAY

I thought all my sins would be blazed out before the great white throne, that every sin committed in childhood and in secret, every secret thought, every evil desire would be declared before the assembled universe, and that everything done in the dark would be brought to light. But thanks be to God, the gospel tells me my sins are all put away in Christ. Out of love for my soul, He has taken all my sins and cast them behind His back. That is a safe place to have sin, behind God's back, because God never turns back. He always marches on. He will never see your sins if they are behind His back. That is one of His own illustrations.

Out of love for my soul, He has taken all my sins upon Him – all, not a part. He takes them all out of the way. There is no condemnation for him who is in Christ Jesus. You may pile up your sins till they rise up like a dark mountain, and then multiply them by ten thousand for those you cannot think of, and after you have tried to enumerate all the sins you have ever committed, let me bring just one verse in, and that mountain will melt away: *The blood of Jesus Christ His Son cleanseth us from all sin* (1 John 1:7). The blood covers the sin.

In Ireland some time ago, a teacher asked a little boy if there was anything that God could not do, and the little fellow said, "Yes. He cannot see my sins through the blood of Christ." That is just what He cannot do. The blood covers them.

Is it not good news to get rid of your sin? You come here a sinner, and if you believe the gospel, your sins are taken away. Believe on the Lord Jesus Christ, and you will be saved. You will be justified from all things, which you could not be by the law of Moses. By believing, or by receiving the gospel, Christ becomes yours. Only think, young man, you are invited to accept the gospel, you are invited to make an exchange, to get rid of all your sins and to take Christ in the place of them. Is not that wonderful?

What a foolish young man you would be not to make the bargain. The Lord says, "I will take your sins and give you Myself in the place of them." But a great many say, "No," and hug the sin to their bosom. May God help you to receive the Lord Jesus Christ as your way, your truth, and your life.

There is another name which used to haunt me a good deal – the great judgment day.

I used to think that it would be a terrible day when I should be summoned before God and could not tell until then whether

I would have a seat on His right hand or on His left. Until I stood before the great white throne of judgment, I could not tell whether I should hear the voice of God saying, "You are cursed, depart from Me," or whether God would say, "Enter into the joy of the Lord." But the gospel tells me that question is already settled. There is now no condemnation for those who are in Christ Jesus.

Listen to this verse: "Verily, verily" – and when you see "verily, verily" in Scripture, you may know there is something very important coming. It means, "Mind what I tell you," or, "truly, truly" – *Verily, verily, I say unto you, He that heareth My Word, and believeth on Him that sent Me, hath* [h-a-t-h, hath – has] *everlasting life, and shall not come into condemnation* [that means, into judgment]; *but is passed from death unto life* (John 5:24).

I am not coming into judgment for sin. The question has been settled because Christ was judged for me and died in my stead, and I go free. Is not that good news?

I heard of a man praying the other day that I might lay hold of eternal life. I could not have said "Amen" to that. I laid hold of eternal life twenty years ago when I was converted. What is the gift of God if it is not eternal life? And that is what God wants to give to everyone, and it is the greatest gift that can be bestowed on any one down here in this dark world. If an angel came straight from the throne of God and proclaimed that God had sent him here to offer to this audience any one thing they might ask, that each one should have his own petition granted, what would be the cry in this audience? There would be but one cry coming up from you, and the shout would make heaven ring – "Eternal life! eternal life!"

Everything would float away into the dim past. There is not anything a man values more than his life. Let a man worth a million sterling be on a wrecked vessel, and if he could just save his life for six months by giving that million, he would give it in an instant. The gift of God is eternal life, and it is one of the greatest marvels that we have to stand and plead and pray for men to take this gift. May God help you to take it now. Do not listen to Satan any longer. Reach out the hand of faith and take it now. Young man, believe on the Lord Jesus Christ, and you will be saved.

Trust Him to save you now, and then there will be no condemnation. Death will have lost his sting, the grave and its victory will be safe out of the way, and the judgment will be past for you. Believe the gospel. Lay hold of eternal life while God is offering it to you. Be reconciled tonight. Take your stand hard by the cross, and you are saved for time and eternity. I am told that in Rome, if you go up a few steps on your hands and knees, that is nine years out of purgatory. If you take one step now you are out of purgatory for time and eternity. You used to have two steps into glory – out of self into Christ, out of Christ into glory. But there is a shorter way now with only one step – out of self into glory, and you are saved.

May God help you to take the step now! Flee tonight to Calvary, my friends, and get under the shadow of the cross.

FIRE ON THE PRAIRIE

Out in our western country, in the autumn, when men go hunting and there has not been any rain for months, sometimes the prairie grass catches fire and there comes a very strong wind, and the flames roll along twenty feet high over that western desert, and go at the rate of thirty or forty miles an hour, consuming man and beast. When the hunters see it coming, what do they do? They know they cannot run as fast as the fire. The fleetest horse cannot escape that fire. Instead, they take a match and light the grass around them and let the flames sweep out, and then they get onto the burnt part and stand safe. They hear the flames roar, they see death coming toward them, but they do not fear, they do not tremble, because the fire has swept over the place where they are, and there is no danger. There is nothing for the fire to burn.

There is one mountain peak that the wrath of God has swept over, and that is Mount Calvary. That fire spent its fury on the bosom of the Son of God. Take your stand here by the cross, and you will be safe for time and eternity. Escape with your life. Flee to that mountain, and you are saved this very minute. Oh, may God bring you to Calvary under the shadow of the cross now! Then let death and the grave come. You will shout, "Glory to God in the highest." We will laugh at death and glory in the grave, and just know this, that we are safe, sheltered by the precious blood of the Lamb. There is no condemnation to him that is in Christ Jesus.

God is coming down and beseeching you to take the pardon. Every man and woman has broken the law, and he that has broken the least of the laws is guilty of all. I am sure I am not talking to one man or woman tonight who can say they have not broken the law.

You have all sinned and come short of the glory of God, but God comes and says, "I will pardon you. Come now, and let us reason together." *Now* is one of the words of the Bible that the devil is afraid of. He says, "Don't be in a hurry. There is plenty of time. Don't be saved now." He knows the influence of that word *now. Tomorrow* is the devil's word. The Lord's word is *now.* God says, *Come now, and let us reason together, saith the Lord: though your sins be scarlet, they shall be as white as snow; though they be red like crimson, they shall be as wool* (Isaiah 1:18). Scarlet and crimson are two fast colors; you cannot get the color out without destroying the garment. God says, "Though your sins be as scarlet and crimson, I will make them as wool and snow. I will do it."

That is the way God reasons. He puts the pardon in the face of the sinner the first thing. That is a queer way of reasoning, but God's thoughts are not our thoughts, and so, my friends, if you want to be saved, the Lord says He will pardon you.

A CHRISTIAN GOVERNOR IN A CONDEMNED MAN'S CELL

A few years ago, when Pennsylvania had a Christian governor, a young man down in one of the counties was arrested for murder. He was brought before the court, tried, found guilty, and sentenced to death. His friends thought there would be no trouble in getting a reprieve or pardon because the governor was a Christian man. They thought he would not sign the death warrant. But he signed it. They called on the governor and begged him to pardon the young man.

But the governor said, "No, the law must take its course, and the man must die." I think the mother of the young man called on the governor and pleaded with him, but the governor stood firm, and said, "No, the man must die."

A few days before the man was executed, the governor took the train to the county where the man was imprisoned. He went to the sheriff and said to him, "I wish you to take me to that man's cell, and leave me alone with him a little while, and do not tell him who l am till I am gone." The governor went to the prison, and talked to the young man about his soul, and told him that although he was condemned by man to be executed, God would have mercy upon him and save him if he would accept pardon from God. He preached Christ, and told him how Christ came to seek and to save sinners, and having explained as best he knew how the plan of salvation, he got down and prayed, and after praying he shook hands with him and bade him farewell.

Sometime later, the sheriff passed by the condemned man's cell, and he called the sheriff to the door of the cell.

He said, "Who was that man that talked and prayed with me so kindly?"

The sheriff said, "That was Governor Pollock."

The man turned deathly pale and threw up both his hands.

He said, "Was that Governor Pollock? Was that kind-hearted man the governor? Oh, sheriff, why did you not tell me? If I had known that was the governor, I would have fallen at his feet and asked for pardon. I would have pleaded for pardon and for my life. Oh, sir, the governor has been here, and I did not know it."

Sinner, I have got good news to tell you. There is one greater than the governor here tonight, and He wants to pardon everyone. He does not want you to go away condemned. He wants to bring you out from under condemnation. He wants to pardon every soul. Will you have the pardon, or will you despise the gift of God? Will you despise the mercy of God? Oh, this night, while God is beseeching you to be reconciled, let me join with your praying mother, with your praying father, with your godly minister, with your Sabbath-school teacher and all your praying friends. Let me join my voice with theirs to plead with you tonight to be reconciled. Make up your mind now that you will not cross your threshold until you are reconciled, and there will be joy in heaven tonight over your decision.

An Englishman told me some time ago a little story of reconciliation, which illustrates this truth. We want to preach the gospel of reconciliation, the good news that God is reconciled. God does not say He can do it, but that He has done it. You must accept what He has done.

The story is this: There was an Englishman who had an only son, and only sons are often petted, and humored and ruined. This boy became very headstrong, and very often he and his father had trouble. One day they quarreled. The father was very angry, and so was the son, and the father said he wished the boy would leave home and never come back. The boy said he would go and would not come into his father's house again till he sent for him. The father said he would never send for him.

Well, away went the boy. But when a father gives up a boy, a mother does not. You mothers will understand that, but the fathers may not. You know there is no love on earth so strong as a mother's love. A great many things may separate a man and his wife. A great many things may separate a father from a son, but there is nothing in the wide world that can ever separate a true mother from her child. To be sure, there are some mothers that have drunk so much liquor that they have drunk up all their affection, but I am talking about a true mother, and she would not cast off her boy.

Well, this mother began to write and plead to the boy to write to his father first, and his father would forgive him. But the boy said, "I will never go home till father asks me." She pleaded with the father, but the father said, "No, I will never ask him."

At last the mother was brought down to her sickbed, broken-hearted, and when she was given up by the physicians to die, the husband, anxious to gratify her last wish, wanted to know if there was anything he could do for her before she died. The mother gave him a look. He well knew what it meant.

Then she said, "Yes, there is one thing you can do, you can send for my boy. That is the only wish on earth you can gratify. If you do not pity him and love him when I am dead and gone, who will?"

"Well," said the father, "I will send word to him that you want to see him."

"No," she said. "You know he will not come for me. If ever I see him, you must send for him."

At last the father went to his office and wrote a message in his own name asking the boy to come home. As soon as he got the invitation from his father, he started off to see his dying mother. When he opened the door to go in, he found his mother dying and his father by the bedside. The father heard the door open and saw the boy, but instead of going to meet him he went to another part of the room and refused to speak to him. His mother seized the boy's hand. How she had longed to press it!

She kissed him and then said, "Now, my son, just speak to your father. You speak first, and it will all be over."

But the boy said, "No, mother, I will not speak to him until he speaks to me."

She took her husband's hand in one hand and the boy's in the other, and spent her dying moments and strength in trying to bring about a reconciliation. Just as she was expiring, she could not speak, so she put the hand of the wayward boy into the hand of the father, and passed away. The boy looked at the mother and the father at the wife and at last the father's heart broke, and he opened his arms and took that boy to his bosom. By that body they were reconciled.

Sinner, that is only a faint type, a poor illustration, because God is not angry with you. God gives you Christ, and I bring you tonight to the dead body of Christ. I ask you to look at the wounds in His hands and feet and the wound in His side. My friends, gaze upon His five wounds. And I ask you, "Will you not be reconciled?"

When He left heaven, He went clear down to the manger that He might get hold of the vilest sinner and put the hand of the wayward prodigal into that of the Father, and He died that you and I might be reconciled. If you take my advice, you will not go out of this hall tonight until you are reconciled. Be reconciled!

Oh, this gospel of reconciliation! My friends, come home tonight. Your Father wants you to come. Say as the prodigal did of old, *I will arise and go to my father* (Luke 15:18), and there will be joy in heaven.

CHAPTER 7

THE WAY OF SALVATION

Read Acts 16:23-40

I have just one thought, and that is to tell every anxious soul what they must do to be "saved." That is the first question of everyone who is honestly and really inquiring into the way of salvation and, God helping me, I will try to make it plain to all.

BEGIN WITH BELIEVING

If I say to you "Believe on the Lord Jesus Christ," you will reply, "Oh, *believe*! I have heard that word till I am sick and tired of it. Scarcely a week but I hear it in the church, or at a prayer-meeting, or at some drawing-room meeting."

You have all heard it over and over again. I don't suppose there is a child over five years of age who cannot repeat that text. What you want is to know how to believe – what it is to believe. Some of you say, "We all believe that Christ came into the world to seek and to save the lost, and that he who believes will be saved."

But the devils believe, and are not saved. They believe and tremble! You must believe *on* the Lord Jesus Christ, and not merely *about* Him, and then you will know what salvation is.

THEN COMES RECEIVING

We will take another word that means the same thing, and perhaps you will get a better hold of it: *He came unto His own, and His own received Him not. But as many as received Him, to them gave He power to become the sons of God, even to them that believe on His name* (John 1:11-12).

Bear in mind, "received *Him*." That's it – not receiving a doctrine or a belief, but receiving Him. It is a person we must receive.

My experience of the last few years is that we all want to have the power before we receive Christ. That is, we want to feel we are in Christ before we will receive Him. But we cannot love God and feel His presence until we have received Him into our hearts. It is just like a boy with a ball. He throws it to you, and you must catch it before you throw it back again. That is the real meaning of "believe." It is "receive," receive Christ as yours. I don't know any verse in the Bible that God has blessed to more souls than John 1:12, *To as many as received Him, to them gave He power.*

I don't know any better illustration than matrimony, for every other illustration doesn't hold good in some points, but I think this is one of the best I could use. Some of you smile at this illustration, but the Bible uses it, and if God uses it in His word, why shouldn't I?

In the Old Testament He uses it in Jeremiah 3:14, *I am married unto you.* Jesus Himself uses it when He speaks of the bride in John 3:29. Paul uses it in his epistles, as in Romans 7:4, as an illustration of the union between Christ and His church. It is an illustration you can all understand, and there is none here that does not know what it means. When a man offers himself, the woman must do either of two things, either receive or reject him. So every soul must do one of these two things – receive or reject Christ.

If you receive Him, that is all you have to do. He has promised power.

There was a shopgirl in Chicago a few years ago, and one day she could not have bought a pound's worth of anything, and the next day she could go and buy a thousand pounds' worth of whatever she wanted. What made the difference? She had married a rich husband. That was all. She had received him and, of course, all he had became hers.

And so, you can have power if you only receive Christ. Remember, you can have no power without Him. You will fail, and fail constantly, until you receive Him into your heart, and I have scriptural authority to say that Christ will receive every soul that will come to Him.

You know that Abraham sent his servant Eliezer on a long journey to get a wife for his son Isaac. When Eliezer got Rebekah, he wanted to be up and off with the young bride, but her mother and brother said, "No, she will wait awhile." When Eliezer was determined to go, they said, "We will inquire of Rebekah." And when Rebekah appeared, they said to her, "Will you go with this man?"

That was a crisis in her life. She could not have said no, but undoubtedly it cost her an effort. It would, of course, be a struggle. She had to give up her parents, home, companions, all that she loved, and go with this stranger. But look at her reply. She said, "I will go."

I am here to get a bride for my Master. "Will you go with this man?" I can tell you one thing that Eliezer could not tell Rebekah. He could not say, "Isaac loves you" because Isaac had never seen his bride. But I can say, "My Master loves you!"

He gave Himself for you. That is love! But bear in mind, my friends, that the moment Rebekah made up her mind to accept Isaac he became everything to her, so that she did not feel she was giving up anything for him. What a mistake some people make! They say, "I'd like to become a Christian if I didn't have to give up so much." Just turn around and look at the other side. You don't have to give up anything, you simply have to receive, and when you have received Christ, everything else vanishes away pretty quick. Christ fills you so that you don't feel these things to be worth a thought.

When a bride marries a man, it is generally love that prompts her. If anyone here really loves a man, is she thinking of how much she will have to give up? No. That wouldn't be love. Love doesn't feed upon itself, it feeds upon the person who is loved. My friends, it is not by looking at what you will have to give up but by looking at what you will receive that will enable you to accept the Savior.

What is Christ to you? What is He willing to be to you if you will have Him? Won't you be made heirs of heaven, joint heirs with Christ to reign with Him for ever and ever, to be His, to be with Him where He is, to be what He is? Think, then, of what He is, and of what He gives. You don't need to trouble yourselves about what you have to give up. Receive Him and all these things will appear utterly insignificant.

I used to think of what I would have to give up. I dearly loved many of the pleasures of this earth, but now I'd as soon go out into your streets and eat the dirt as do those things. God doesn't say, "Give up this and that." He says, "Here is the Son of my bosom – receive Him." When you do receive Him, everything else goes.

Stop that talk about giving up. Let Christ save you, and all these things will go for nothing. Mark the words from John 1:12, *To as many as received Him, to them gave He power.* Now, my friends, will you go with this man? You have often heard about Christ. You know as much about Him as anyone here perhaps, but did you ever know a man or woman who regretted receiving Him? No man ever regretted receiving Christ, but I have heard of thousands who have been followers of the devil and have regretted it bitterly.

And I notice that it is always the most faithful followers of the devil who regret it most.

Take Jesus. My friends, accept my advice, and take Jesus with you. Remember, He is the gift of God offered to whosoever. You belong to that class, don't you? Just take Him. That's the first thing you have to do. When you go to cut down a tree, you don't take the axe and commence to hew down the branches. No, you begin right down at the root. So here, you must take Christ, and then you will get power to resist the world, the flesh, and the devil.

THE EXAMPLE OF RUTH AND ORPAH

Another case is Ruth and Orpah. Many are like these two young widows. A crisis had come in their lives. Both had lost their husbands and were living in the mountains of Moab. Often had they visited the graves of their dear ones, perhaps planted a few flowers there and watered them with their tears. Naomi, their mother-in-law, is about to return to her native land, and they think they will travel part of the way with her. It is a sad parting, but now the crisis comes. Down in the valley they embrace each other and give the parting kiss, and they both say they will go with Naomi, but she warns them of the difficulties and the trials that might await them.

Orpah says, "I will go back to my people," but Ruth cannot leave her mother-in-law and says she will go with her.

Orpah turns back alone, and I can see her on the top of the

hill. She stops and turns round for a last look. And Naomi says to Ruth, "Your sister-in-law has gone back to her people, and to her gods. Go back with her."

What does Ruth say? "Do not ask me to leave you or to return and not follow you, for wherever you go, I will go, and where you stay, I will stay. Your people will be my people and your God my God."

Her choice was made. Poverty here or suffering and want there, she would share Naomi's lot.

Orpah loved Naomi but not enough to leave all for her, while Ruth loved her mother-in-law so much that leaving her people seemed nothing to her. Oh, may God draw out all your hearts, so that you may leave all and follow Him! We never hear any more of Orpah. The curtain falls on her life. Perhaps she died away in the mountains of Moab, without God and without hope. But how different with Ruth! She becomes famous in history. She is one of the few women whose names have come down through the ages, and she is brought into the royal line of heaven. I have an idea that God blessed her for that decision, and He will bless you if you decide in a like manner. Who will say tonight, as Ruth did, "I will follow you, and your God will be my God"? Will anyone take up the language of Ruth? Is there not a Ruth here? If there is, the Master is calling.

INTRODUCING THE CONCEPT OF TRUSTING

I'll take another word. I have been speaking of *receive*, but the next word I want your attention for is *trusting*. Many understand that when they cannot get hold of *believe* or *receive*. You all know what it is to trust. If it were not for trust, there would be a terrible commotion in this building tonight. If you could not trust that the roof was firmly put up, you would get out pretty quick, and if you could not trust these chairs to support you, how long would you sit on them? You wouldn't have come here at all if you didn't trust our word that there would be an address.

This is the same trust that God wants, not a miraculous trust or faith, but the same kind, only the object is different. Instead of trusting in these earthly things, or in an arm of flesh, you are asked to trust in the Son of God.

In Dublin I was speaking to a lady in the inquiry room when I noticed a gentleman walking up and down in front of the door. I said, "Are you a Christian?" He was very angry and turned on his heel and left me. The following Sunday night I was preaching about receiving, and I put the question, "Who will receive Him now?" That young man was present, and the question sank into his heart. The next day he called on me – he was a merchant in that city – and said, "Do you remember me?"

"No, I don't."

"Do you remember the young man who answered you so roughly the other night?"

"Yes, I do."

"Well, I've come to tell you I am saved."

"How did it happen?"

"I was listening to your sermon last night, and when you asked, 'Who'll receive Him now?' God put it into my heart to say, 'I will,' and He has opened my eyes to see His Son."

I don't know why thousands should not do that here tonight. If you are ever to be saved, why not now?

But another point you must remember: Salvation is a free gift, and it is a free gift for us. Can you buy it? It is a free gift, presented to "whosoever." Suppose I were to say, I will give this Bible to "whosoever." What have you got to do? Why, nothing but take it. But a man comes forward, and says, "I'd like that Bible very much."

"Didn't I say 'whosoever'?"

"Yes, but I'd like to have you say my name."

"Well, here it is."

Still he keeps eyeing the Bible and saying, "I'd like to have that Bible, but I'd like to give you something for it. I don't like to take it for nothing."

"I am not here to sell Bibles. Take it if you want it."

"Well, I want it, but I'd like to give you something for it. Let me give you a penny for it, though it is certainly worth twenty or thirty shillings."

Suppose I took the penny, and the man takes up the Bible, and marches away home with it. His wife says, "Where did you get that Bible?"

"Oh, I bought it."

This is the point: When he gives the penny it ceases to be a gift. So with salvation. If you were to pay ever so little, it would not be a gift.

"TRYING" IS USELESS

Man is always trying to do something. This miserable word *try* is keeping thousands out of heaven. When I hear men speak of trying, I generally tell them it is the way down to death and hell. I believe more souls are lost through trying than any other way. You have often tried and as often failed, and as long as you keep trying you will fail. Drop that word and take as your sure foothold for eternity the word *trust*. Job said, "Though He slay me, yet I will trust Him," and that is the right kind of trust. Would to God that everyone would say, "I will trust Him now, tonight." Did you ever hear of anyone going down to hell trusting in Jesus? I never did. This very night, if you commit yourself to Him, the battle will be over.

You are complaining you don't feel better. Remember, the child must be born before it can be taught. So we cannot learn of God until we receive Him. We must be born – born again, the new birth – before we can feel. Christ must be for us the hope of glory. How can He be in us if we don't receive Him and trust Him?

Another verse that has been used a great deal during the past two years, and I feel that I rest my own salvation on, is John 5:24. I trust God will write it on your hearts and burn it into your souls. *Verily, verily, I say unto you, He that heareth My Word, and believeth on Him that sent Me, hath everlasting life, and shall not come into condemnation; but is passed from death unto life.* Thank God for that "hath."

I had a few men in the inquiry room the other night who could not find peace. I said, "Do you believe the Bible?"

"Yes, sir."

"I think I will prove you don't. Turn to John 5:24." They turned there. "Read the verse."

"He that heareth My Word ..."

"You believe that?"

"Yes, sir. 'And believeth on Him that sent me ...'"

"'You believe God sent Jesus?"

"Yes."

"Read on."

"Hath everlasting life."

"You believe you have everlasting life?"

"No, we don't."

"Oh, so you don't believe the Bible!"

What right have you to cut a verse in two and say you believe the one half but not the other? It plainly says that he who believes "hath everlasting life, and shall not come into condemnation; but is passed from death unto life." If you believe God's words, you can say, "I have passed from darkness into light." Just by resting on that one little word in the present tense we may have assurance now. We don't need to wait till we die and till the great day of judgment to find it out.

A lady in Glasgow came to me and said, "Mr. Moody, you are always saying 'Take, take!' Is there any place in the Bible where it says 'take,' or is it only a word you use? I have been looking in the Bible for it but cannot see it."

"The Bible is sealed with it," I said. "It is almost the last word in the Bible": *And the Spirit and the bride say, Come. And let him that heareth say, Come. And let him that is athirst come. And whosoever will, let him take the water of life freely* (Revelation 22:17).

"Well," she said, "I never saw that before. Is that all I have to do?"

"Yes. The Bible says so." And she took it, then and there.

God says, "Let him take," and who can stop us if God says it? All the devils in hell cannot hinder a poor soul from taking, if God says, "Take." My friends, are you going to "take" tonight? Are you going to let these precious meetings pass without getting Christ, without being able to look up and say, "Christ is my Savior, God is my Father, heaven is my home"?

A lady came to my house the other night, anxious about her soul, but after some conversation she left without finding peace. She came again, and I asked, "What is the trouble?"

"I haven't got peace."

I took her to this verse, *He that believeth on the Son hath everlasting life* (John 3:36). I just held up that little word *hath* to her, and turned to John 5:24, and 6:47. There these words were spoken by Jesus, and they are all linked to believing on the Son. After we had talked for some time, she looked in my face earnestly, and said, "I have it!" and went away rejoicing in the Savior's love.

If you seek life, you can have it now as you sit upon your seat. The word *hath* occurs again in Isaiah 53:6, *All we like sheep have gone astray; ... and the Lord hath laid on Him the iniquity of us all.* Our iniquity has been laid upon Christ, and the Lord is not going to demand payment twice. *Who His own self bare our sins in His own body on the tree* (1 Peter 2:24).

Suppose I owed Mr. Wanamaker a thousand pounds, and I became a bankrupt. I would have nothing to pay, so he might send me to prison. But suppose Mr. Stone heard of it and says, "I don't want to see Moody taken to prison." So he pays the debt for me and gets the receipt. When I see the receipt, I know that I am free. But Mr. Wanamaker finds out that I didn't pay it and gets me hauled off to court. He says he must have me pay it myself, or I must go to prison. I show the receipt.

"The debt is paid," says the judge.

Mr. Wanamaker says, "Moody didn't pay it."

Would any judge in the land support him? No. It is paid and cannot be demanded again. If man does not ask payment twice, will God? Certainly not! The case is this: The debt has been paid, and our sins have been atoned for. Christ Himself has redeemed us, not with corruptible things, such as silver and gold, but with His precious blood. Therefore we are free. But remember, although salvation is free for us, it cost God a great deal to redeem us. He had an only Son, and He gave Him up freely for us.

What a wonderful gift! If you make light of so great a salvation, how can you escape the damnation of hell?

SETTLE THE GREAT QUESTION

Now, one question: What are you going to do with Christ? You have got to answer that question. You may get angry, like a man a short time ago who marched out of a church saying, "What right has that American to make such a statement?" But it is true, and you must answer it. Pilate wanted to shirk the responsibility and sent Jesus to Herod, but he was forced to a decision. When the Jews forced him to decide, he washed his hands and said he was innocent of this man's blood. But did that take away his guilt? No.

An angel may be here, hovering over this audience, and he is listening to what is said. Someone may say, "I will receive Him. I will delay no longer." Immediately, the angel will wing his way right up to the pearly gates and tell the news that another sinner has been saved. There will be a new song ringing through the courts of heaven over sinners repenting. God will issue the command to write down their names in the book of life and to get rooms ready for them in the new Jerusalem, where we all will soon be.

A man was once being tried for a crime for which the punishment was death. The witnesses came in one by one and testified to his guilt but there he stood, calm and unmoved. The judge and the jury were quite surprised at his indifference. They could not understand how he could take such a serious matter so calmly. When the jury retired, it did not take them many minutes to decide on the verdict of guilty, and when the judge was passing the sentence of death upon the criminal, he told him how surprised he was that he could be so unmoved at the prospect of death.

When the judge had finished, the man put his hand in his bosom, pulled out a document, and walked out of the dock a free man. That was how he could be so calm. It was a free pardon from his king, which he had in his pocket the whole time. The king had instructed him to allow the trial to proceed and to produce the pardon only when he was condemned. No wonder, then, that he was indifferent as to the result of the trial.

That is just what will make us joyful in the great day of judgment. We have a pardon from the Great King, and it is sealed with the blood of His Son.

After the Chicago fire, a great many things were sent to us from all parts of the world. The boxes they came in were labeled, "For the people who were burned out," and all a man had to do was to prove that he had been burned out, and he got a share. So here, you have but to prove that you are poor, miserable sinners, and there's help for you. If every man who is ruined and lost will cling to *try*, there is no hope; but if he gives it all up as a bad job, then Christ will save him. The law condemns us, but Christ saves us.

The superintendent of a Sabbath school in Edinburgh was walking down the street one day when he met a policeman leading by the hand a little boy who was crying bitterly. He stopped and asked the policeman what was the matter with the boy.

"Oh," said the officer, "he has gotten lost."

The superintendent asked to look at him. They went to a lamp and held up the little boy. In a moment the boy knew his superintendent and flew to his arms. The gentleman took him from the policeman, and the boy was comforted. The law has got us but let us flee into Jesus' arms and we are safe.

A friend of mine in the North told me of a poor Scottish lassie who was very anxious about her soul. He told her to read Isaiah 53. She replied, "I canna read, and I canna pray. Jesus, take me as I am!" That was the true way, and Jesus just took her as she was. Let Him take you this night, just as you are, and He will receive you into His arms.

One night, when preaching in Philadelphia, right down by the side of the pulpit there was a young lady whose eyes were riveted on me as if she were drinking in every word. It is precious to preach to people like that.

After I was finished preaching, I spoke to her.

"Are you a Christian?"

"No, I wish I was. I have been seeking Jesus for three years."

I said, "There must be some mistake."

She looked at me, confused, and said, "Don't you believe me?"

"Well, no doubt you thought you were seeking Jesus, but it doesn't take an anxious sinner three years to meet an anxious Savior."

"What am I to do, then?"

"The matter is, you are trying to do something. You must simply believe on the Lord Jesus Christ."

"Oh, I am sick and tired of the word *believe, believe, believe!* I don't know what it is."

"Well," I said, "we'll change the word. Take *trust*."

"If I say I'll trust Him, will He save me?"

"No, I don't say that. You may say a thousand things, but if you do actually trust Him."

"I do trust Him, but," she added in the same breath, "I don't feel any better."

"Ah, I've got it now! You've been looking for feelings instead of Jesus for three years. Faith is up above, not down here."

People are always looking for feelings. You are preparing a new translation of the Bible here, and if the men who are translating it would only put in feelings instead of faith, what a rush there would be for that Bible. But if you look from Genesis to Revelation, you cannot find feelings attached to salvation. We must rise above feelings.

So, I said to this lady, "You cannot control your feelings. If you could, what a time you'd have! I know I would never have the toothache or the headache."

FEELINGS ARE THE DEVIL'S TOOL

Feelings are the last plank the devil sticks out just as your feet are getting on the rock of ages. He sees the poor trembling sinner finding his way to the Savior, and when he shoves out this plank the poor sinner thinks he's all right now.

Some sermon you have heard arouses you, but then you feel all right when you get on this plank. Six months after, perhaps, you are dying, and the devil comes along when you think you're quite safe.

"Ah," he tells you, "that was my work. I made you feel good."

And where are you then? But take your stand on God's word and you cannot fail. His word has been tried for six thousand years, and it has not failed.

So I said to the lady, "Have no more to do with feelings but, like Job, say, 'though He kill me, yet I will trust in Him.'"

She looked at me a few minutes, and then, putting her hand out to take mine, she said, "Mr. Moody, I trust the Lord Jesus Christ to save my soul tonight."

Then she went to the elders and said the same words. As she left, she met one of the church officers and, shaking his hand, said again, "I trust the Lord Jesus to save my soul."

Next night she was right before me again. I shall never forget her beaming face. The light of eternity was shining in her eyes! She went into the inquiry room. I wondered why she was going there, but when I arrived, I found her with her arms around a lady friend, saying, "It's only to trust Him. I have found it so." From that night she was one of the best workers in the inquiry room and whenever I met a difficult case, I got her to speak to the person, and she was sure to help them.

Surely you can trust God tonight. You must have a very poor opinion of God if you cannot trust Him. You have only to come to Him this way – receive Him and trust Him. What more can you do, and what less can you do than trust Him? Is He not worthy of it? Let us be perfectly still for a moment, and while the voice of man is hushed, let us think of one passage of Scripture: *Behold, I stand at the door and knock* [that is Christ standing at the door of your heart, knocking, and He says,] *if any man hear My voice, and open the door, I will come into him, and will sup with him, and he with Me* (Revelation 3:20).

Will anyone tonight pull back the bolts and say, "Enter, you are three times welcome. Blessed Savior, come in." God grant that all who hear may do this!

CHAPTER 8

THE EIGHT "I WILLS" OF CHRIST

*Come unto me, all ye that labour and are heavy
laden, and I will give you rest. Take my yoke upon
you, and learn of me; for I am meek and lowly in
heart: and ye shall find rest unto your souls.*
– Matthew 11:28-29

I wish to call your attention to the eight "I wills" of Christ.
The first one you will find in Matthew 11:28-29.

ONE: I WILL GIVE YOU REST

I never met a person that did not want rest. The man or woman
that doesn't want rest is not living on the face of the earth. We
read of the rich man, who was going to pull down his barns and
build larger ones, saying to his soul, "Take your ease, there is
plenty laid up in store, so now take your rest." Merchants work
day and night to amass money in order that they may rest.
Men leave their families and friends and go around the world
to earn money in the hope that they may get rest. Sailors plow

the sea and are away from home for months to get money in order that it may bring them rest.

In fact, if rest could be bought in the market, there are many hundreds in London who would be paying a very high price for it. Though money can't buy it, by believing the word of God you can nevertheless get it without money and without price. Jesus says, "Come to Me, all you who labor and carry heavy burdens, and I will give you rest.

When we say "we will," it often doesn't mean much. Perhaps we don't intend to keep our word when we say we will do a thing or, if we do mean to keep it, we very often fail for want of ability to make our promise good. But bear in mind, God never breaks His promise, He never makes a mistake, and He never fails to fulfill His word. The words I have read may be relied on, for they are not the words of man but of the Son of God – "Come unto Me, all you that labor and are heavy-laden, and I will give you rest."

This tells us of the only place where we can find rest. There is no other place where a man can possibly find rest for his soul. Bear this in mind: It is not coming to some creed, it is not coming to some particular church, or to some particular doctrine, but to Christ: "Come to Me." It is coming to a personal Christ that alone gives peace and rest to the soul.

John 14:27 holds a promise that is very precious to me: *Peace I leave with you, my peace I give unto you: not as the world giveth, give I unto you. Let not your heart be troubled, neither let it be afraid.* Christ says, "Peace I leave with you."

"I am going away," he says, "but I am not going to take away My peace from you. That I leave behind Me. My peace I give to you." Mark that little expression "My peace." A good many people look for peace from worldly sources, but when they find it they don't get much out of it for the devil can play on men's feelings as men play on a harp and can delude them into almost anything. But if we go to Christ for it, we get what we want. We get rest for the soul and, until we go to Him, we will never get it.

A good many things disturb our peace, but nothing can disturb the peace of God. You might take this little island and throw it right into the Atlantic, and it would make a great stir and commotion in this world, but I don't think that God would be moved on His eternal throne. It would not disturb Him in the heavens, high and lifted up above all the earth. Let us have the peace of God, and then we shall have rest.

Again He says, *These things have I spoken unto you, that my joy might remain in you* (John 15:11). Christ's joy, not our joy. When we come to a personal Christ, and our souls are stayed on Him, then we get rest and peace and joy. That is a rest that nothing can disturb. It is peace that flows on like a river, and that is joy forever more.

TWO: I WILL NOT CAST YOU AWAY

The next "I will" is in John 6:37. I can imagine some of you people saying, "If I were only good enough to come, I would come and get this rest and peace and joy." But if you read that verse, you will find it says, *Him that cometh to Me I will in no wise cast out.*

Surely that is broad enough, isn't it? I don't care who the man or woman is. I don't care what your trials, what your troubles, what your sorrows, or what your sins are, if you will only come straight to the Master, He will not cast you out. Come then, poor sinner, come just as you are and take Him at His word.

A wild and prodigal young man came into one of our meetings. He was running a headlong career to ruin, but the Spirit of God got hold of him. While I was conversing with him and trying to bring him to Christ, I quoted this verse to him. I held it right up to him and led his mind right up to it for some time and, at last, light seemed to break in upon him. He seemed to take comfort from it, so I told him to stick to that verse.

After he left, on his way home, the devil met him. I don't believe that any man ever starts to go to Christ but the devil strives somehow or other to meet him and trip him up, and even after he has come to Christ the devil comes and tries to assail him with doubts and make him believe there is something wrong in it. And so, this young man was met by Satan, who whispered to him, "How do you know that is a right translation?"

That brought him to a standstill and threw him into darkness again. But he remembered my telling him to stick to that text, and there he was, after Satan had put that into his mind, holding on to it, but he did not find peace till two o'clock, when he said to himself, "I will stick to it anyhow, and if it is not the right translation, when I get to the bar of God I will tell Him I didn't know it was wrong, because I didn't understand anything about Greek and Latin."

"Him who comes to Me I will in no way cast out." If you will only come to Him, I have good authority to tell you that Christ will receive you today – in fact, this very hour.

The kings and princes of this world, when they issue invitations, call to themselves the rich, the mighty and powerful, the honorable and the wise, but the Lord, when He was on earth, called around Him the vilest of the vile. "This man," they said in Luke 15, "receives sinners and eats with them." Publicans, sinners, and harlots pressed into the kingdom of God in His days.

Here in London, there is no society that would have such a man in their company as John Bunyan once was, yet the Lord saved him and welcomed him into His kingdom. Here was a poor, miserable drunkard cast out by his father and mother and deserted by all his friends, but the Lord received him. I have known some of the most miserable outcasts that were ever seen, cast out and despised by everybody, and yet the Lord has received them. Take Him then at His word today, and accept His invitation, "He who comes to me I will not cast out."

But, you say, I must get rid of my sins first, and then I will come to Him. That's just like a man dying of the scarlet fever saying, "I'll wait till I get rid of the fever before I send for a doctor!" It is because you are a sinner and cannot get rid of your sins that you need a savior. If I were dying for want of bread, it would be just as reasonable for me to say, "When I have got rid of this hunger, then I will begin to eat." It is because I am hungry that I need to eat, and it is because we are sinners that we need Christ. It is because a man is sick that he needs a physician, and Christ is the Physician of the soul.

THREE: I WILL MAKE YOU CLEAN

In Luke 5 we read of the leper coming to Christ for healing and the Lord saying to him, *I will: be thou clean. And immediately the leprosy departed from him* (Luke 5:13).

That's another "I will" I want to call your attention to. If there is any man or woman here full of the leprosy of sin, if you will but go to the Master and tell all to Him, He will speak to you as He did to that poor leper, and say "I will. Be clean." The leprosy of your sins will fly away from you. It is the Lord, and the Lord alone, who can forgive sins. There is His word, just look at it again: "I will: be thou clean," and then put that with the other verse, "Him that cometh to Me I will in no wise cast out."

One day, when Whitfield was preaching, he said the Lord was so anxious to save souls that He would take in the devil's castaways. Lady Huntingdon protested and said he ought not to make such statements. A little while after, however, a poor, fallen woman, an outcast from society, came to his preaching. She was laboring under a deep conviction of sin, and before long she found peace in her Savior and was received into the kingdom of God. If there is a poor sinner here, let him take this one verse and then keep in his mind on that poor leper coming to Christ. The law forbade him to come, but Christ is above the law. *For the law was given by Moses, but grace and truth came by Jesus Christ* (John 1:17).

You can make a wonderful exchange today. You can have health in the place of sickness, and you can get rid of everything that is vile and hateful in the sight of God. The Son of God comes down and says, "I will take away your leprosy, and give you health in its stead. I will take away that terrible disease that is ruining your body and soul and give you my righteousness in its stead. I will clothe you with the garments of salvation."

Isn't this a wonderful thing? That's what He means when He says, "I will." Lay hold of this "I will!"

FOUR: I WILL CONFESS YOU TO MY FATHER

Turn to Matthew 10:32: *Whosoever therefore shall confess me before men, him will I confess also before my Father which is in heaven.* This is the "I will" of confession. That's the next thing that takes place after a man is saved. We have been washed in the blood of the Lamb, and the next thing is to open our mouths. We have to confess Christ here in this dark world and tell His love to others. We are not to be ashamed of the Son of God.

A man thinks it a great honor when he has achieved a victory that causes his name to be mentioned in Parliament, or in the presence of the Queen and her court. A very great honor. And in China, we read, the highest ambition of the successful soldier is to have his name written in the palace or temple of Confucius. But just think of having your name mentioned in the kingdom of heaven by the Prince of Glory, by the Son of God, because you confess Him here on earth. You confess Him here,

He will confess you there. If you wish to be brought into the clear light of liberty, you must take your stand on Christ's side.

I have known many Christians who grope about in darkness and never get into the clear light of the kingdom because they were ashamed to confess the Son of God. Don't be ashamed, Christians, to let your friends, and even your enemies, know that you are on God's side.

FIVE: THE "I WILL" OF SERVICE

There are a good many Christians here, I believe, who have been aroused to say, "I want to do some service for Christ." Well, Christ says, *Follow Me, and I will make you fishers of men* (Matthew 4:19). There is no Christian who cannot help to bring someone to the Savior. Christ says, *And I, if I be lifted up from the earth, will draw all men unto me* (John 12:32), and our business is just to lift up Christ, and live to Him. You may go on preaching like the angel Gabriel, but if you live like a devil, your preaching goes for nothing. I do not care how eloquent you are, and what beautiful language you use, your preaching goes for nothing. It is no good following this man or that man. Follow Christ and Him only. He says, "I will make you fishers of men."

Peter had a good haul on the day of Pentecost. I doubt if he ever caught so many fish in one day as he did men on that day. It would have broken every net they had on board if they had to drag up three thousand fishes. Our Lord said, "Follow Me, Peter, and I will make you a fisher of men," and Peter simply obeyed Him, and there, on that day of Pentecost, we see the result.

But there is one reason, and a great reason, why so many do not succeed. I have been asked by a great many good men, "Why is it we don't have any results? We work hard, pray hard, and preach hard, and yet success does not come." I will tell you:

It is because a good many people spend all their time mending their nets. No wonder they never catch anything.

By holding inquiry meetings, and thus pulling the net in, you can see if you have caught anything. If you are always mending and setting the net, you won't catch many fish. Whoever heard of a man going out to fish, setting his net and then letting it stop there, and never pulling it in? Everybody would laugh at the man's folly.

A minister in Manchester came to me one day and said, "I wish you would tell me why we ministers don't succeed better than we do." I brought before him this idea of pulling in the net, and I said, "You ought to pull in your nets. There are many ministers in Manchester who can preach much better than I can, but then I pull in the net." Many people have objections to inquiry meetings, but I urged upon him the importance of them, and the minister said, "I never did pull in the net. I will try next Sunday." He did so, and eight people, anxious inquirers, went into his study. The next Sunday he came down to see me and said he had never had such a Sunday in his life. He had met with a marvelous blessing. The next time he drew the net there were forty, and when he came to see me at the Opera House the other day, he said to me joyfully, "Moody, I have had eight hundred conversions this last year! It is a great mistake I did not begin earlier to pull in the net." So, my friends, if you want to catch men, just pull in the net.

If you only catch one, it will be something. It may be a little child, but I have known a little child convert a whole family. You don't know what's in that little dull-headed boy in the inquiry room. He may become a Martin Luther, a reformer who will make the world tremble. You cannot tell. God uses the weak things of this world to confound the mighty. God's promise is as good as a Bank of England note: "I promise to pay So-and-so." Here is one of Christ's promissory notes: "If you follow Me, I will make you fishers of men." Won't you lay hold of the promise and trust it and follow Him now?

But then, if you wish to catch men, you must use a little – what shall I say? – common sense.

That's the plain English of it. If a man preaches the gospel and preaches it faithfully, he ought to expect results then and there. But after he has proclaimed the glad tidings, let him have an inquiry meeting, and, if necessary, a second meeting, and go to the people's houses and talk and pray with them, and in that way hundreds will be brought to God. I believe it is the privilege of God's children to reap the fruit of their labor three hundred and sixty-five days in the year.

"But," somebody might say, "is there not a time to sow as well as harvest?"

Yes, it is true, there is, but you can sow with one hand and reap with the other. What would you think of a farmer who went on sowing all the year round and never thought of reaping? I repeat, we want to sow with one hand and reap with the other, and if we look for the fruit of our labors, we will see it. "If I be lifted up, I will draw all men unto Me." We must lift Christ up, seek men out and bring them to Him. You must use the right kind of bait. A good many people don't do this, and then they wonder why they are not successful. You see them getting up all kinds of entertainments with which to try and catch men. They work the wrong way around. I will tell you what this perishing world wants: It wants Christ, and it wants Him crucified.

In every man's bosom there is a void that needs filling, and if we only approach them with the right kind of bait we shall catch them. This poor world needs a Savior, and if we are going to be successful in catching men, we must preach Christ crucified – not His life only, but His death. If we are faithful in doing this we shall succeed. And why? Because there is His promise: "If you follow Me, I will make you fishers of men." And that promise holds just as good for you and me as it did to His disciples and is as true now as it was in their time. *And they that be wise shall shine as the brightness of the firmament; and they that turn many to righteousness as the stars for ever and ever* (Daniel 12:3).

Think then of the exalted privilege of turning one soul to Christ. You set a stream in motion that will run for ages after you are gone. Revelation 12:3 says those who die in the Lord will rest from their labors and their works will follow them.

Think of Paul up there. People are going up every day and every hour, men and women who have been brought to Christ through his writings. He set streams in motion that have flowed on for more than a thousand years. I can imagine men going up there and saying, "Paul, I thank you for writing that letter to the Ephesians. I found Christ in that." "Paul, thank you for writing that epistle to the Corinthians." "Paul, I found Christ in that epistle to the Philippians." "I thank you, Paul, for that epistle to the Galatians. I found Christ in that."

And so, I suppose, they are going up still, thanking Paul all the while for what he has done. When Paul was put in prison, he did not fold his hands and sit down in idleness. No, he began to write. His epistles have come down through the long ages of time and brought thousands on thousands to a knowledge of Christ crucified. Yes, Christ said to Paul, "I will make you a fisher of men if you will follow Me," and he has been fishing for souls ever since. The devil thought he had done a very wise thing when he got Paul into prison, but he was very much mistaken. He overdid it for once. I have no doubt Paul has thanked God ever since for that Philippian jail and his stripes and imprisonment there. I am sure the world has made more by it than we shall ever know till we get to heaven.

SIX: I WILL NOT ABANDON YOU

The next "I will" is in John 14:18: *I will not leave you comfortless: I will come to you.*

To me it is a sweet thought that Christ has not left us alone in this dark wilderness here below. Although He has gone up on high and taken His seat by the Father's throne, He has not left us. The better translation is, "I will not leave you orphans." He did not leave Joseph when they cast him into prison. God was with him. When Daniel was cast into the den of lions, they put the Almighty in with him. They were so bound together that they could not be separated, and God went down into the den of lions with Daniel.

There is no separation between us. If we have got Christ with us, we can do all things. Do not let us think how weak we are. Let us lift up our eyes to Him and think of Him as our Elder Brother who has all power given to Him in heaven and on earth. He says, "I am with you, even to the end of the world."

Some of our children and friends leave us, and it is a very sad hour when some member of our family goes to a distant country, perhaps to Australia. But thank God, the believer and Christ shall never be separated. He is with us here, and we shall be with Him in person by and by. We shall be with Him and see Him in His beauty. Not only is He with us, but He has sent us the Holy Ghost, who will tell us all things. Let us honor the Holy Ghost by acknowledging that He is here in our midst. He has the power to give sight to the blind and liberty to the captive and to open the ears of the deaf that they may hear the glorious words of the gospel.

SEVEN: I WILL RAISE HIM UP

This "I will," in John 6:40; occurs four times in the chapter: *I will raise him up at the last day.*

It is very sweet to think that I have a Savior who has power over death. My blessed Master holds the keys of death and hell. I pity the poor unbeliever and the poor infidel. They have no hope of resurrection. But every child of God can open that chapter and read the promise, and his heart ought to leap for joy as he reads it.

You know, the tradesman generally puts the best of his wares in the window to show us the quality of his stock, and when Christ was down here, He gave us a sample of what He could do. He raised three from the dead that we might know what power He had. There was Jairus's daughter, the widow's son, and Lazarus of Bethany. He raised all three of them so that every doubt might be swept out of our hearts. How dark and gloomy this world would be if we had no hope in the resurrection but now, when we lay our little children down in the grave, although it is in sorrow, it is not without hope. We have seen them pass away, we have seen them in the terrible struggle with death, but there has been one star to illuminate the darkness and gloom – the thought that though the happy circle has been broken on earth, it shall be completed again in the world of heavenly light.

You that have lost a loved one rejoice as you read that "I will." Those who have died in Christ will come forth again. The darkness shall flee, and the morning light of the resurrection will dawn upon us. It is only a little while, and He who has said it will come, His voice will be heard in the grave, *I will raise him up at the last day.* Precious promise! Precious "I will!"

EIGHT: I WILL BRING YOU INTO MY GLORY

Next is the "I will" of glory, from John 17:24: *Father, I will that they also, whom thou hast given me, be with me where I am.*

That was in His last prayer before He went into the garden on the last night before He was crucified and died that terrible death on Calvary. I see some here whose countenances begin to light up at the thought that they will be with the King in His beauty by and by. There is a glorious day before us in the future. Some think that on the first day they are converted they have got everything. To be sure, we get salvation for the past, and peace for the present, but there is the glory for the future. That's what kept Paul rejoicing. He said, "These light afflictions, these few stripes, these few brickbats and stones that they throw at me, the glory that is beyond excels them so much that I count them as nothing, nothing at all, so that I may win Christ." And so, when things go against us, let us cheer up. Let us remember that the night will soon pass away and the morning will dawn.

Death never goes there. It is banished from the heavenly land. Sickness, pain, and sorrow do not come to mar the grand and glorious home where we will be with the Master. God's family will be all together there. It is a glorious future, my friends! A glorious day! And it may be a great deal nearer than many of us think. During these few dark days we are here, let us stand steadfast and firm, and by and by we will be in the unbroken circle in the world of light, and the King will be in our midst.

THE "I WILL" OF THE SINNER

And now there is just one more "I will," which I want you to say, and that is the "I will" of the sinner. You have the eight "I wills" of Christ:

1. He will give us rest.

2. He will not cast out the vilest but will receive all that come.

3. He will make us clean.

4. He will confess us as His.

5. He will make us successful winners of souls.

6. He will not leave us comfortless.

7. He will raise us up at the last day.

8. He wills that we be with Him in glory.

And now I want sinners to say, "I will arise and go to my father."

Who will say it this afternoon? Who will come to God as the poor prodigal did? I can see him now. Perhaps he is looking over those blue hills, and away in the distance he can see the home he has left. He knows that a loving, gray-headed father is there, and he says, "I am dying here in a foreign land while there is bread enough to spare in that home which I have left. I will rise and go to my father."

That was the turning-point in the prodigal's life. That was a glorious thing to do, wasn't it, sinner?

When Mr. Spurgeon preached the other day in the West End, he summed up the things his audience had "gotten over." Some of you, he said, have gotten over the prayers of faithful Sunday School teachers who used to weep over you and come to the house and talk to you. You resisted all their entreaties, and you have gotten over their influence. And you have gotten over your mother's tears and prayers, and she, perhaps, sleeps in the grave today. You have gotten over the tears and prayers of your father and of your minister, who has prayed with you and wept with you, a godly, faithful minister. There was a time when his sermons took hold of you, but you have gotten over them now, and his sermons make no impression. You have been through special meetings, and they have made no impression on you, they have not touched you.

Still, you say, you are getting on. So you are, but bear in mind that you are getting on as fast as you can to hell, and there is not one man in ten thousand who can hope to be saved after he has grown so hard-hearted.

My friends, say, "I will rise!" Let there be joy in heaven today over your return. We read in Luke 15 that there is joy in heaven over one sinner who repents. May many return now, and live.

FROM THE HYMN "I WILL GO"

I am lost, and yet I know
    Earth can never heal my woe;
I will rise at once and go,
    Jesus died for me.

CHAPTER 9

THE RIGHT KIND OF FAITH

Sirs, what must I do to be saved? – Acts 16:30

I do not know of any truth more important to bring out than the answer to this question, because this is the beginning of everything with regard to the divine life. A man must know he is saved before there is any peace or joy or comfort. The answer to the question is, *Believe on the Lord Jesus Christ, and thou shalt be saved* (Acts 16:31), and the question that comes right after that, from almost everyone, is, "What does it mean to believe?"

I believe that Jesus Christ is the Son of God. I believe that He came into the world to save sinners. Well, so do the devils, who not only believe but tremble. I can believe intellectually that Jesus Christ is able and willing to save and yet be as far from the kingdom of God as any man who never heard about Jesus Christ. Believing that He can and is willing to save you by itself won't save you. I will now take up the word "faith," which means believing.

People ask, "What is faith?" The Bible definition of faith is perhaps as good as anyone that we know of. We are told in

Hebrews, *Now faith is the substance of things hoped for, the evidence of things not seen* (Hebrews 11:1). So, faith is – what? The substance or the "ground" or "confidence." In other words, faith is dependence upon the veracity of another. All business is carried out on this principle of faith. If men lose confidence in one another, see how quickly business could cease here in London. Let men withdraw their confidence and see what would take place in the commercial world tomorrow. It was faith that brought you here. If you had not faith to believe that there would be a meeting in this hall, you would not have come.

Somebody has said that there are three things about faith – knowledge, assent, and taking hold, and it is the last that is safe. Not the knowledge. A great many people say, "I believe Christ is able to save." They give their assent, and say, "I believe," but that does not save. It is that last verb, the taking hold, that saves, and that is what we want to press upon you.

Faith has an outward look, not an inward one. Hundreds of people spend time looking at their own hearts, but faith looks outward.

FINDING WHERE TO PUT YOUR FAITH

We are to have faith in God and not in man. Many people place their faith in men, pinning their faith to other people's doctrines and creeds. Not long ago I heard of a man who was asked what he believed. He said he believed what his church believed.

"What does your church believe?"

"The church believes what I believe."

And that was all they could get out of him. A great many people are in that same state of mind. They believe what the church believes, but they do not know what the church believes. If their church teaches it, they believe it. All the churches in the world can't save a soul. It is not to have faith in this church or that church, this doctrine or that doctrine, this man or that man, but it is to have faith in the man Christ Jesus, who sits at the right hand of God. That is the only faith that will ever save a soul.

Let me call your attention to a few verses where God has warned us not to put faith in man, Jeremiah 17:5-7: *Thus saith the Lord; Cursed be the man that trusteth in man, and maketh flesh his arm, and whose heart departeth from the Lord. For he shall be like the heath in the desert, and shall not see when good cometh; but shall inhabit the parched places in the wilderness, in a salt land and not inhabited. Blessed is the man that trusteth in the Lord, and whose hope the Lord is.*

You will find some men who do not have faith in God, and they are like a tree that is withered and blasted. And perhaps there is a man right along next to him who has strong faith in God: *He is like a tree planted by the rivers of water; his leaf also shall not wither* (Psalm 1:3). Why? Because he trusts in the living God. *Happy is he that hath the God of Jacob for his help, whose hope is in the LORD his God* (Psalm 146:5). Cursed is the man that leans on an arm of flesh and trusts in man.

The same thought is brought out in Isaiah 30, *Woe to the rebellious children, saith the Lord, that take counsel, but not of me; and that cover with a covering, but not of my Spirit, that they may add sin to sin: that walk to go down into Egypt, and have not asked at my mouth; to strengthen themselves in the strength of Pharaoh, and to trust in the shadow of Egypt! Therefore shall the strength of Pharaoh be your shame, and the trust in the shadow of Egypt your confusion* (Isaiah 30:1-3).

In one place He says "woe" and in another place He says, "Cursed be the man." It is a terrible thing for man to put faith in man. Again, in Psalm 146:3-5, *Put not your trust in princes, nor in the son of man, in whom there is no help. His breath goeth forth, he returneth to his earth; in that very day his thoughts perish. Happy is he that hath the God of Jacob for his help, whose hope is in the Lord his God.* Here we are told very plainly by God that we are not to put our trust in this man or that man, not to lean on an arm of flesh. All the ministers in the world and all the potentates in the church put together cannot save one soul. It is thoroughly impossible. It is the Lord that can save, and the Lord alone, and therefore we want to get our eyes away from man, from the church, and put them on the man Christ Jesus.

Mark 11:22 tells us in whom we are to believe, and how sweet it sounds: *And Jesus answering saith unto them, Have faith in God.* I never saw a man or woman in my life who had faith in God and was confounded. I do not care what their troubles or trials were. Have faith in God and not in man.

SINCERITY IS THE GREAT DELUSION

We are living in very strange days. Some people tell us it does not make any difference what a man believes – if he is only sincere. One church is just as good as another – if you are only sincere. I do not believe any greater delusion ever came out of the pit of hell than that. It is ruining more souls at the present time than anything else. I never read of any men more sincere or more earnest than those men at Mount Carmel, those false prophets who were so terribly in earnest.

Some might say, "If these men are holding, as you say, error, why should they be so earnest?" Those prophets of Baal were some of the most earnest men I ever read of. You do not read of men now being so earnest that they take knives and cut themselves. Look at them leaping upon their altars; hear their cry, "O Baal! O Baal!" We never heard that kind of prayer on this platform. They acted like madmen. They were terribly in earnest, yet did God hear their cry? They were all slain.

"I believe one religion is just as good as another, if you are only sincere in what you believe." This is one of the devil's lies.

Have faith in God, not in man. I don't care how good a man is, don't put your faith in him. His breath leaves him, he dies, and where is your help? Our God never dies. Our God never will disappoint us if we put our faith in Him. "Have faith in God," says Christ.

Some time ago, I saw some men trying to go up in a balloon fastened to their car. They had one rope fastened, but by some mistake that rope got untied, and instead of seizing hold of the car they seized hold of the rope. One of them let go. The other just hung on, and he was swept away into the heavens and was lost.

"It did not make any difference. If he had hung on to the car, it would have been just the same," you say, "if he was only sincere." That man was very sincere when he seized hold of that rope, yet he was lost. He perished in his earnestness. My friends, bear in mind that if you do not believe on the Lord Jesus Christ you must perish. It is God who says it, not man. Some may say, "He is such a good man, I can't help but believe him. It is all right because he is such a good man, and he holds that doctrine."

But Paul says that if anyone preaches any other gospel than what you have received from us, let him be cursed. If Gabriel should come right down here tonight, and commence to proclaim a different gospel from this platform, I would get out of the hall and would not listen to him.

DECEIVERS DARKEN THE DAYS

People are out in the world who would deceive even the very elect if they could. I believe we are living in dark days. Error is coming in on all sides, and it is a time when we must maintain the faith. "I have kept the faith," says Paul. The good old doctrine of our forefathers and of the Puritans is a good deal better than this new doctrine that does away with Christ, with hell, and even with heaven. Let us cling to the word of God and have faith in God.

God sent a young man down to Bethel and told him to prophesy against it. He was not to eat and drink in the place, nor to go back by the same way as he went. Down the young man went. The king asked him to go to his palace, but he refused. God had told him to go and prophesy, not to eat and drink. But there was an old prophet, and he sent word to the young man that an angel had told him to invite him, and the young man obeyed the voice of the angel rather than God. When he started home, a lion met him and slew him. We are not to put our faith in this man or that man, not even in a prophet if it is contrary to the word of God. Do not believe the best man living if it is contrary to the word of God.

If God says it, let us take our stand on it. God's word will still be standing when these men and their names have been swept away and forgotten. There have always been false teachers, men trying to teach us it does not make any difference what a man believes if he is only sincere. My friends, let us have faith in the living God, and then there will be light where it is now darkness.

FAITH COMES THROUGH KNOWING GOD

Turn to John 20. I can imagine some of you saying, "I would like to have faith in God, but I do not know how to get it. I have been praying a long time for faith." I used to pray, "O God, give me faith," and yet I was all the time neglecting the Bible, but it tells us how we are to get faith: *But these are written, that ye might believe that Jesus is the Christ, the Son of God; and that believing ye might have life through His name* (John 20:31).

John took up his pen and wrote the gospel for one express

purpose. What was it? That men might believe that Jesus Christ was the Son of God. Every chapter but two in John speaks of believing, and if you run through the gospel and mark the word *believe*, you would find out why that gospel was written. It is, "Believe, believe, believe, believe." It keeps focused on that one thing. He took up his pen and wrote his gospel that we might believe, and by believing we get life.

Now turn to Romans 10:15-17: *How shall they preach, except they be sent? as it is written, How beautiful are the feet of them that preach the gospel of peace, and bring glad tidings of good things! But they have not all obeyed the gospel. For Esaias saith, Lord, who hath believed our report? So then faith cometh by hearing, and hearing by the word of God.*

Do you want to know how to get faith? It is to get acquainted with God. Job is told, *Acquaint now thyself with him, and be at peace* (Job 22:21). We find the people who are best acquainted with God have the most peace. People that do not know God do not trust Him. The people who know God put their trust in Him. I never knew a man who was well acquainted with God who did not trust Him. The more you know of a man who is true the more you trust him. I met a man ten years ago for the first time, and I did not put much faith in him because I did not know much about him. In the course of a year, I got well acquainted with him and found him to be true. Then I had more faith in him. The second year I had still more, and this year I have more faith in him than ever because I know him well now. If you know God you cannot help trusting Him.

Some time ago, I wanted to teach my little boy what faith was, so I put him on a table. He was a little fellow, two years old. I stood back three or four feet and said, "Willie, jump."

The little fellow said, "Pa, I'm afraid."

I said, "Willie, I will catch you. Just look right at me and jump."

He got all ready to jump and then looked down again, and said, "I'm still afraid."

"Willie, didn't I tell you I would catch you? Will Pa deceive you? Now, Willie, look me right in the eye and jump, and I will catch you."

He got ready to jump the third time, but he looked on the floor, and said, "I'm afraid."

"Didn't I tell you I would catch you?"

"Yes."

At last I said, "Willie, don't take your eyes off me." I held his eyes, and I said, "Now jump. Don't look at the floor," and he leaped into my arms.

Then he said, "Let me jump again."

I put him back, and the moment he got on the table, he jumped, and after that, when he was on the table and I was standing five or six feet away, I heard him cry, "Pa, I'm coming," and had just time to rush and catch him. He seemed to put too much confidence in me.

But you cannot put too much confidence in God. Faith never looks down. It looks right up. God says, "Trust me," and God will bring us through all our difficulties, if we will only trust Him. Who will trust Him tonight? Who will have faith in Him tonight? *Whatsoever He saith unto you, do it* (John 2:5) is what the mother of Christ said at the wedding, and whatsoever God speaks to you, do it. If God tells you to run, run. If God says, "Believe," believe, and you will always be safe in doing just what God tells you to do.

UNBELIEF IS THE GREATEST ENEMY

I have a great admiration for the old woman who said that if God told her to jump through a stone wall she would jump. Getting through the wall was God's work, not hers, and she would do whatever God told her to do. The greatest enemy God and man have is unbelief. Christ found it on both sides of the cross. It was the very thing that put Him to death. The Jews did not believe Him, did not believe God had sent Him, and they took Him to Calvary and murdered Him.

The first thing we find after He got up out of the grave was unbelief again. Thomas, one of His own disciples, did not believe He had risen. Jesus said, "Thomas, feel these wounds," and Thomas did and believed and said, "My Lord and my God." Those Christians here that have learned to trust God will bear me out in this, that the more they know of God, the more they can trust Him. Why? They have found God to be true. When man has failed, God has never failed, and when everyone else has disappointed them, God has proved true.

Now, you who have never trusted Him, won't you just leap right into His arms tonight? Won't you just take Him at His word, and believe on Him now?

UNBELIEF IS THE GREATEST INSULT TO GOD

It is considered that the greatest insult you can offer a man is to call him a liar. Unbelief is telling God that He is a liar. Suppose a man said, "Mr. Moody, I have no faith in you whatever." Don't you think it would grieve me? There is not anything that would wound a man much more than to be told that you do not have any faith in him.

Many men say, "I have profound reverence and respect for God." Yes, profound respect, but not faith. It is a downright insult! Suppose a man says, "Mr. Moody, I have profound respect for you, profound admiration for you, but I do not believe a word you say." I wouldn't give much for his respect or admiration. I wouldn't give much for his friendship. God wants us to put our faith in Him.

How it would wound a mother's feelings to hear her children say, "I do love mama so much, but I don't believe what she says." How it would grieve that mother. And that is about the way a great many of God's professed children talk. Some men seem to think it is a great misfortune that they do not have faith, but bear in mind that it is not a misfortune – it is the damning sin of the world.

GOD ALWAYS KEEPS HIS WORD

Is there any reason why you should not have faith in God? Has God ever broken His word? I will defy any infidel to come forward and put his finger on any promise God has ever made to man that He has not kept. I can show you how for six thousand years the devil has lied, and how he has broken every promise he has made. What a lie he told Adam and Eve, and yet I can more quickly find a thousand men who will believe one of the devil's lies than I can find one man that believes God's truth. Men will believe lies, but when it gets to real truth, how few will believe the word of God.

Why should not every man and woman in this house have faith in God? Why should not everyone put confidence in Him now, and trust God to save them? And let me say, if you are ever saved, you will have to come to this one point of trusting to God for salvation. You will never be saved until you put your trust and confidence in God.

Look at John 3:33: *He that hath received his testimony hath set to his seal that God is true.* In those days men used to wear a signet ring with their initials, and instead of signing their names they used the ring to seal the document. That was "setting to their seal." It was an endorsement. And now God comes down into this unbelieving world, and says, "Who will set to his seal that I am true?"

I want to ask the friends in this hall, "Who will set to his seal or her seal that God is true?" It is a great deal better for us to make ourselves liars and God true than to try and make ourselves out to be true and God a liar. That is what many men will do. Who will set his seal to the proposition that God is true? Unbelief says, "I won't." Faith says, "I will."

Oh, may God help many now to say this very hour, "I will set my seal that God is true," and, my friends, the moment you do and put your faith in God, then comes the peace, the happiness you have been looking for so long!

THERE IS NO PEACE WITHOUT TRUST

Many people will look for peace and happiness before they will trust. There will be no peace, no happiness, no joy, until you put your trust in God. The joy that flows through the Christian's heart is the result of trusting God.

Suppose I meet a man tonight leaping for joy, laughing at the top of his voice. I say, "My friend, what makes you so happy?"

"I don't know. I am so happy I cannot contain my feelings!"

What would you say? Why, you would say the man had gone mad. But suppose I meet a man whom I have seen out here night after night begging, and I say to him, "Hello, beggar, is that you?"

"Don't call me a beggar. I am no longer a beggar."

"Are you not the man who has been begging here every night?"

"Yes."

"Where did you get your good clothes? How is this that you are not a beggar?"

"I am no beggar. I am worth a thousand pounds."

"How is that?"

"Well, sir, last night I was here begging, and a man came along and put a thousand pounds in my hand."

"How did you know it was good money?"

"I took it to the Bank of England, and they gave me gold for it."

"How was it done?"

"I just held out my hand, and he came and put a check right into it, and I took it to the bank and got gold for it."

"Did you really get it in that way?"

"Yes."

"How do you know it was the proper signature?"

"What do I care about the signature?" says the beggar. "I have the money."

Faith is the hand that reaches out and takes the blessing. Any faith that brings me to Christ is the right kind of faith, and instead of looking at your faith, look to Christ. Someone has said that faith sees a thing in God's hand and says, "I will have it." Unbelief sees it and says, "God won't give it to me."

Look to God by faith tonight and have salvation.

Who will have it? Every man and woman may have it if they will but put their trust in God. Is God not worthy of our confidence? Is God not worthy of our trust? You must have a poor opinion of God if you cannot trust Him. We think we have a poor opinion of a man if we cannot trust him, and if a man should tell me something, and I did not believe a word he said, I would have a very poor opinion of that man.

Faith is putting confidence in God's word. Take hold of His word tonight. He will save all who will come, and not only that, but He will save you when you do come. Do away with everything but Christ and take Him now. Who will take God at His word tonight?

Someone has said, "Faith is saying yes to God." Who will say yes tonight and take it? Is it too much to ask or to expect that every person in this hall should put their faith in God? If God does not save us, who will? Men cannot save us, the church cannot, creeds and doctrines cannot. Sacraments cannot save.

Baptism cannot save. You must have a living personal Christ, and God presents Him to the world. Who will take Him? Who will have Christ – who will trust Him? Faith says, "I will." Isn't it the very best thing you can do? Can you do a better thing than trust God for salvation?

"What must I do to be saved?" Believe on the Lord Jesus Christ, or trust the Lord Jesus Christ for salvation, and trust Him now.

It is recorded in history of a man who was condemned to death that when he came to lay his head on the block the prince asked him if there was any one petition that he could grant him. All the condemned man asked for was a glass of water. They got him a tumbler of water, and when he got it his hand trembled so that he could not get it to his mouth. The prince said to him, "Your life is safe until you drink that water." He took the prince at his word and dashed the water to the ground. They could not gather it up, and so he saved his life.

My friends, you can be saved tonight by taking God at His word. The water of life is offered to "whosoever will." Take it now, and live. *So then faith cometh by hearing, and hearing by the word of God* (Romans 10:17).

Faith is not what we see or feel. It is, simply, trust in what a God of love has said about Jesus the Just.

CHAPTER 10

THE DYING THIEF

And one of the malefactors which were hanged
railed on him, saying, If thou be Christ, save thyself
and us. But the other answering rebuked him, say-
ing, Dost not thou fear God, seeing thou art in the
same condemnation? And we indeed justly; for we
receive the due reward of our deeds: but this man
hath done nothing amiss. And he said unto Jesus,
Lord, remember me when thou comest into thy
kingdom. And Jesus said unto him, Verily I say
unto thee, Today shalt thou be with me in paradise.
– Luke 23:39-43

I am going to take as my text a man who was the last one
saved before Christ went to heaven, or before He died on
the cross, and the story of his conversion ought to give hope to
every man. We have an account of the conversion of all classes
of people in the Bible. Not one class is left out. There are the
richest and the poorest, the greatest and the smallest – all classes
of men and all classes of women.

There are so many people nowadays talking against sudden conversions that I think the very best thing we can do is to see what the Scripture says about it – to see how long it takes God to convert a soul. If I read my Bible correctly, there were eight thousand converted in two days. That was a good number in a short time, was it not? We have not reached that yet. I wish we had, but I feel sure that if the church of God would only wake up, we should see something like it.

IT IS NEVER TOO LATE

This man was not only a thief but a reviler of God, right upon the threshold of eternity, a most depraved and abandoned wretch. Matthew tells us: *The thieves also, which were crucified with him, cast the same in his teeth* (Matthew 27:44). You would have thought they would have something better to do than that, coming so near death and the grave, and that their thoughts would have been very solemn in the face of not only death but, after death, the judgment. Instead of that, they reviled Christ and cast accusations in His teeth a few hours before their death. I do not think this thief could have sunk any further until he sank into hell, though that is how far down Jesus found him.

Matthew and Mark both tell us that these two thieves reviled Him. John says nothing about this and, in fact, he does not tell us about one of them being converted. The first we get of it is in Luke 23:40, where we find him saying to the other thief, *Dost not thou fear God?* Solomon, the wise man, says, "The beginning of wisdom is the fear of God." Here we have the beginning of wisdom in this thief. He began to fear God, and I hope there will be hundreds in this building who will fear Him, for that truly is the beginning of wisdom.

The next thing, the man was convicted. No man is likely to be converted until he is first convicted of sin, and this thief was convicted. What convicted him? He heard no sermon from Christ. The rulers were then deriding Him. The chief men of His own country had found Him guilty of blasphemy and had condemned Him to die the death of the cross. The chief men of the realm were there wagging their heads and mocking Him. What was it then that convicted this poor thief? He had seen Christ perform no miracles. He had heard no wonderful words fall from His lips, and he saw no glittering crown upon His brow.

True, it was written over His cross, "Jesus, the King of the Jews," but where was His kingdom? He saw none of the Jews paying homage to Him. The Jews were putting Him to death and there was no scepter in His hand. True, He had been crowned a little while before, but only with thorns, and yet amid it all this poor thief was convicted after fear fell upon him.

LOVE HAS POWER

What convicted him? I will tell you what I think convicted him, though I could not teach it dogmatically but I think it was the Savior's prayer. When the Lord Jesus cried out from the very depths of His soul, "Father, forgive them," conviction flashed into his heart. He must have said, "This is more than a man. He has a very different spirit from me. I could not ask God to forgive them. I would call down fire from heaven to consume them, and I would call upon God to smite them with blindness as Elijah did, and I would sweep them from this mountain if I had the power." That's what he must have thought as he heard the piercing cry go up, "Father, forgive them, for they know not what they do."

It was love that broke his heart. In those days, when they crucified a man, they used to scourge him. This poor man had been taken into the court and tried and condemned by the judge, but that had not broken his heart. He had been led out and scourged, but that had not broken his heart. And now they had nailed him to the cross, and even that had not broken his heart. There he is reviling his God, but when he saw that loving Savior, he got a glimpse of His love, and that one glimpse broke his heart.

I heard of a young man once who was very hardhearted. His father loved him as he loved his own life. He had tried everything he could to win that prodigal boy back. When his father was dying, they sent for him, but he refused to come, and after his father's death, he returned home to attend the funeral, but not a tear fell from his eyes. He followed his father to his resting place and never dropped a tear over his grave. But when they got home, and the will was read, they found that father had not forgotten his prodigal boy, but had remembered him kindly in his will, and this proof of the father's love just broke his heart.

And so I think it must have been with the thief when he heard the Savior crying, "Father, forgive them for they know not what they do." It was an arrow piercing his heart, and he was convicted.

CONFESSION FOLLOWS CONVICTION

The next point for this man was that he confessed his sin. He says to his brother thief, "We are suffering justly – we deserve it." I never knew a man who was saved until he took his stand as a sinner. Cain never confessed his sin. Judas never confessed his sin to God, though he went and confessed it to man. I want to say that I am not here to urge you to confess your sins to any man unless you have done some sin against him and he is stumbling over it. If so, go and confess that, certainly. Otherwise, we must not confess our sins to anyone but God. I have not much sympathy with the class of people that are always running to this man and that man to confess their sins. There is no priest on earth that can forgive sins. I have a high priest who is "a priest forever after the order of Melchizedek." The only man that Scripture tells us confessed his sins to man was Judas, and he went right out and hung himself.

THE THIEF PUTS HIS FAITH IN CHRIST

The next thing about this thief was his faith in Christ Jesus. We talk about the faith of Abraham and Moses, but this thief had the most remarkable faith of any man on record. He took his stand at the very head of the class, passing by many who had wonderful faith. He heard no sermon, saw no scepter in Christ's hand, no crown on His brow, nor witnessed any marvelous works, yet he had wondrous faith.

God was twenty-five years toning up Abraham's faith. God met Moses in the burning bush and went up into the mountains and talked with him, and Isaiah saw God lifted up on His throne, but not so with this thief. There were many who had met Christ and seen wonderful things. His disciples had heard Him speak and had seen Him raise the dead and yet they had forsaken and left Him. Yet here amid the darkness and gloom, this poor thief put his faith in Him. Although his hands and feet were nailed to the cross, his eyes were not, and he could look at Him. They did not nail his heart to the cross, and it is with the heart that man believes, as we read in Romans, and with his heart the thief believed. There is faith for you.

HE WAS NOT ASHAMED OF CHRIST

The next thing was that he confessed Christ at that dark period, the darkest hour of Christ's pilgrimage down here. We will never see another hour as dark as that. The sin of the world was on Him, and heaven was closed against Him – locked, bolted, and barred. He was hanging on the tree bearing our sins, *for it is written, Cursed is every one that hangeth on a tree* (Galatians 3:13). Even God had to hide His face from Him, for He could not look on sin, and Christ was then bearing the sin of all the world. I believe that's what Christ meant in the garden of Gethsemane when He prayed that the cup might pass from Him. Up to that time He saw His Father's face, and He knew He was blessed of Him, and from time to time a voice came from heaven, "This is my beloved Son."

But now He was taking our place before God as a sinner, and God had to hide His face from Him. Yes, it was breaking the Savior's heart, and now, when darkness was coming over creation, the moon would be turned into blood, and the sun was about to veil its face because it could not look upon the terrible scene. Peter, one of His most conspicuous disciples, had denied Him with a curse, and swore that he never knew Him, and Judas, another of His own disciples, had gone out and sold Him for thirty pieces of silver, and the chief men of the nation were mocking Him, saying, "He saved others, let Him save Himself if He is the Christ."

In the middle of all this darkness and gloom, out from the thief comes this sign of faith, "Lord, remember me." He called Him Lord there and then, and he said to the other thief, "This man has done nothing wrong." Thank God for that confession. There's faith and confession for you. If you want to be saved, you must have faith in Christ and be ready to confess Him before all men.

Look at the prayer of the thief. People say, "Pray for salvation, and you will get it!" Yes, but bear in mind you must have faith in Christ before you can pray. This thief had faith in Christ, and now he called Him "Lord." It was the sound of a young convert's voice, *Lord, remember me when thou comest into thy kingdom* (Luke 23:42). It was not a very long prayer, but it was red-hot and right out of his heart. Some people tell you they cannot pray without a prayer book, but the poor thief had none, and if there had been any prayer books then, there was nobody to give him one. He wanted salvation. He simply wanted to be saved, and he cried from his heart, "Lord, remember me!" and a more eloquent prayer never was heard or printed on earth. But not only that, he got more than he asked, for he only asked to be remembered. We always get more than we ask when we come to the Lord.

THE WORLD TAKES ITS LAST LOOK AT CHRIST

When a great man dies, people are very anxious to get his last words and acts, and it is sweet to have the last words of the Son of God. The last sight the world had of Christ was on the cross. They have never seen Him since. We have no record that any uncircumcised eye beheld Christ after He rose from the dead. The last glimpse the world had of Christ was saving a poor sinner as he hung on the cross, saving him from the jaws of hell and the grasp of Satan. Christ snatched him out of the very grasp of the devil, and said to him, *This day shalt thou be with me in paradise* (Luke 23:43).

The lion of the tribe of Judah conquered the lion of hell when He snatched the dying thief as a lamb out of Satan's grasp. "This day you will be with me in paradise." That's the glorious gospel, free from the law. There is no condemnation to them that are in Christ Jesus.

In the days of Wilberforce, when slavery was abolished, it was said that no slave could live under the Union Jack because a bill had been passed declaring every man free. The news went abroad, and when the captain of a ship was going to a distant island in the slave dominions, the negroes were watching for the news to see if it was true. They were anxious to know if the bill had passed and they were really free, and when the captain came in sight of the little island, they were waiting to get the tidings. The captain put his trumpet up to his mouth and shouted across the island, "Free! Free!," and the cry was taken up and echoed through the island, "Free! Free!" They shouted for joy, because they were slaves no longer.

I bring you good news. The Son of God will speak the word *free*. He spoke the words on the cross, and the poor thief was a free man. Satan could not hold him.

Think of the contrast! In the morning, he was led out a poor condemned man, cursing and reviling the Son of God Himself, and in the evening he was singing the new song of redemption. That evening I see him hard by the throne, singing the sweet song of Moses and the Lamb. In the morning cursing, in the evening singing, "Glory to God in the highest." Wasn't that a change? What a contrast! Think of it, oh sinner. Condemned in the morning by man, cast out as too vile for earth, and in the evening good enough for heaven, in the evening washed in the blood of the Lamb, and Christ ready to receive him into the kingdom of heaven.

Christ was not ashamed to walk down the crystal pavement of heaven with him. The thief heard the shout on the cross when Christ called out, "It is finished!" How his soul must have thrilled with joy at that shout! He said, "My salvation is completed now." He saw the spear thrust into that side and the blood flow out, and I can see the sparkle on his face lit up with glory. "Without the shedding of blood there is no remission." It was a sad sight, but glorious.

THE BEST THING TO DO IS YIELD

Young man, do you want Him to save you? Are you ready to confess Him as your Lord and Savior? Take your stand by the Master and say, "From this hour, I will serve the Lord Jesus!"

If so, it will be the best night in your life up to this time. The best thing you can do is to yield to Christ at once. Every true Christian would give you that advice, and if I could shout clear up to the throne, and ask the Savior what He would have you to do, I would hear a voice rolling down from heaven saying, "Tell him to seek salvation." When the thief was converted, it was probably the first time he had ever heard of the Lord Jesus Christ. But it is surely not so with you.

How many people keep putting salvation off and off until it is one day too late! There are so many who live in the future. It is better you should be wise and enter into the kingdom of God now. Let your prayer, like that of the thief, go up from your heart, "Lord, remember me." You will not ask in vain.

A MINER'S TIMELY CONVERSION

A minister in Edinburgh tells a story of the conversion of a young man who was working in one of the mining districts. When the meeting at one of the churches was over on a particular evening, the minister saw him standing by a pillar in the church, the rest having gone out, all but two or three, and they asked this man if he was going home. He said, "I have made up my mind that I will not leave this church till I become a Christian." So, they stopped and talked and prayed with him. That man did the best thing he could do. I would like every man here to do the same thing. Make up your minds that you won't leave till you have settled your soul for eternity.

The next day, while this young man was working in the mine, the coal fell in on him, and before he died, he had just strength enough left to say to his companions, "It's a good thing that I settled it last night – a very good thing." Young man, I will leave you to answer the question: Was it not a good thing he settled it that night?

A young man who was in the army during the Civil War told me that when he heard that his brother, from whom he had never been separated, had joined a certain regiment, he went right away and put his name down under his brother's. They ate together, marched together, and fought shoulder to shoulder. At last his brother was struck with a minié ball, and he fell mortally wounded by his side. He saw too plainly that he must die and, as the battle was raging and he could do nothing to save him, he put his brother's knapsack under his head and made him as comfortable as he could. Bending over him, he kissed him, bade him good-bye and left him to die. As he was going away, his brother said, "Charlie, come back, and let me kiss you upon your lips."

"As I bent over him," said the young soldier who told me the story, "he kissed me on my lips, and said, 'Take that home to mother, and tell her that I died praying for her,' and as I turned away from him, I could hear him say, as he lay weltering in his blood, 'This is glory.' I wondered what he meant, I asked him what was glory. He said, 'Charlie, it's glorious to die looking up. I see Christ in heaven.'"

DIE LOOKING UP

If you want to die looking up and seeing Christ, seek the kingdom of God. You may never hear the call again. Do not leave this place without making up your mind to settle the solemn question of eternity.

DWIGHT L. MOODY
- A BRIEF BIOGRAPHY

Dwight Lyman Moody was born on February 5, 1837, in Northfield, Massachusetts. His father died when Dwight was only four years old, leaving his mother with nine children to care for. When Dwight was seventeen years old, he left for Boston to work as a salesman. A year later, he was led to Jesus Christ by Edward Kimball, Moody's Sunday school teacher. Moody soon left for Chicago and began teaching a Sunday school class of his own. By the time he was twenty-three, he had become a successful shoe salesman, earing $5,000 in only eight months, which was a lot of money for the middle of the nineteenth century. Having decided to follow Jesus, though, he left his career to engage in Christian work for only $300 a year.

D. L. Moody was not an ordained minister, but was an effective evangelist. He was once told by Henry Varley, a British evangelist, "Moody, the world has yet to see what God will do with a man fully consecrated to Him."

Moody later said, "By God's help, I aim to be that man."

It is estimated that during his lifetime, without the help of television or radio, Moody traveled more than one million miles, preached to more than one million people, and personally dealt with over seven hundred and fifty thousand individuals.

D. L. Moody died on December 22, 1899.

Moody once said, "Some day you will read in the papers that D. L. Moody, of East Northfield, is dead. Don't you believe a word of it! At that moment I shall be more alive than I am now. I shall have gone up higher, that is all – out of this old clay tenement into a house that is immortal; a body that death cannot touch, that sin cannot taint, a body fashioned like unto His glorious body. I was born of the flesh in 1837. I was born of the Spirit in 1856. That which is born of the flesh may die. That which is born of the Spirit will live forever."

OTHER SIMILAR TITLES

Moody's Addresses
by Dwight L. Moody

Where am I? Who am I? Where am I going? I think it is good for a man to pause and ask himself these questions. I do not ask you where you are in the eyes of your family, friends, or the community in which you live. It is of very little account what men think of us, but it is of vast importance what God thinks of us.

Am I in communion with my Creator or out of communion? If I am out of communion, there is no true peace, joy, or happiness. But when we are in communion with God, there is light all around our path. You may think that your life is hidden, that God does not know anything about you, but He knows our lives much better than we do, and His eye has been fixed on us from our earliest childhood until now.

Available where books are sold.

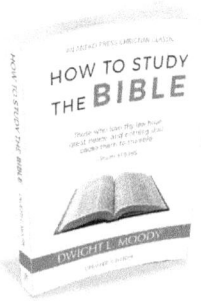

How to Study the Bible
by Dwight L. Moody

There is no situation in life for which you cannot find some word of consolation in Scripture. If you are in affliction, if you are in adversity and trial, there is a promise for you. In joy and sorrow, in health and in sickness, in poverty and in riches, in every condition of life, God has a promise stored up in His Word for you.

This classic book by Dwight L. Moody brings to light the necessity of studying the Scriptures, presents methods which help stimulate excitement for the Scriptures, and offers tools to help you comprehend the difficult passages in the Scriptures. To live a victorious Christian life, you must read and understand what God is saying to you. Moody is a master of using stories to illustrate what he is saying, and you will be both inspired and convicted to pursue truth from the pages of God's Word.

Available where books are sold.

www.ingramcontent.com/pod-product-compliance
Lightning Source LLC
Chambersburg PA
CBHW061756120626
46550CB00005B/2022